"The title says it all: representing C [barcode] others outside it—which is to say, participating in the royal priesthood of believers—is the great privilege and responsibility of every Christian. Anizor and Voss rightly call attention to this important theme, explaining its Christocentric-Trinitarian grounding, its biblical unfolding from Adam to Christ and its historical development, especially its recovery by Martin Luther at the time of the Reformation. They also call for a recovery of the royal priesthood in the contemporary church and the seven priestly practices that are vital to the church's ministry and mission. This is a fine example of theology retrieval for the sake of church renewal."

Kevin J. Vanhoozer, research professor of systematic theology, Trinity Evangelical Divinity School

"*Representing Christ* provides both a historical and theological framework for understanding this almost forgotten concept, the priesthood of all believers. Anizor and Voss offer a masterful analysis and application of priesthood that is rooted deeply in the Scriptures. Their reflections of both clerical and lay priesthood situate this idea as a connection between liturgy as worship and mission. Their christocentric-trinitarian paradigm also provides practical suggestions for local churches to live out the call to priesthood in the fullest sense of missio Dei. *Representing Christ* will be required reading for my students and should be for all those committed to participating in the work of Christ's priesthood in the church and world."

Elizabeth Gerhardt, professor of theology and social ethics, Northeastern Seminary

"Having fallen precipitously from watchword to buzzword, 'the priesthood of all believers' is in dire need of recovery today. Anizor and Voss rescue it from disuse, misuse and abuse and restore it to its proper place: under the high priesthood of Christ, in relation to the Triune God and in service to the world. This book guards a precious doctrine against hierarchical errors on one side and democratic errors on the other. Readers who have come to think of priesthood as a marginal topic or none of their business will find the theme expanding here to such vast and comprehensive proportions that it begins to seem like the main thing the Bible is about."

Fred Sanders, professor of theology, Torrey Honors Institute, Biola University

REPRESENTING CHRIST

A Vision for the
Priesthood of All Believers

UCHE ANIZOR & HANK VOSS

IVP Academic

An imprint of InterVarsity Press
Downers Grove, Illinois

InterVarsity Press
P.O. Box 1400, Downers Grove, IL 60515-1426
ivpress.com
email@ivpress.com

InterVarsity Press® is the book-publishing division of InterVarsity Christian Fellowship/USA®, a movement of students and faculty active on campus at hundreds of universities, colleges and schools of nursing in the United States of America, and a member movement of the International Fellowship of Evangelical Students. For information about local and regional activities, visit intervarsity.org.

Scripture quotations, unless otherwise noted, are from The Holy Bible, English Standard Version, copyright © 2001 by Crossway Bibles, a division of Good News Publishers. Used by permission. All rights reserved.

While any stories in this book are true, some names and identifying information may have been changed to protect the privacy of individuals.

Portions of chapters two and three contain revised material from Uche Anizor, Kings and Priests: Scripture's Theological Account of Its Readers *(Pickwick, 2014). Used by permission of Wipf and Stock Publishers, www.wipfandstock.com.*

Cover design: Cindy Kiple
Interior design: Beth McGill
Images: Jordan's Quaker Meeting by Rod Waddams. Private Collection / Bridgeman Images

ISBN 978-0-8308-5128-7 (print)
ISBN 978-0-8308-9974-6 (digital)

Printed in the United States of America ∞

Library of Congress Cataloging-in-Publication Data
Names: Anizor, Uche, 1976- author. | Voss, Hank, 1976- author.
Title: Representing Christ : a vision for the priesthood of all believers /
  Uche Anizor and Hank Voss.
Description: Downers Grove, IL : InterVarsity Press, 2016. | Includes
  bibliographical references and index.
Identifiers: LCCN 2016007921 (print) | LCCN 2016009332 (ebook) | ISBN
  9780830851287 (pbk. : alk. paper) | ISBN 9780830899746 (eBook)
Subjects: LCSH: Priesthood, Universal.
Classification: LCC BT767.5 .A55 2016 (print) | LCC BT767.5 (ebook) | DDC
  234—dc23
LC record available at http://lccn.loc.gov/2016007921

P	20	19	18	17	16	15	14	13	12	11	10	9	8	7	6	5	4	3	2	1
Y	33	32	31	30	29	28	27	26	25	24	23	22	21	20	19	18	17	16			

Dedicated to

Zoe, Eli and Ezra

Samuel, David, Renée and Isaiah

May you represent Christ with joy as you

share in his royal priesthood

CONTENTS

ACKNOWLEDGMENTS

WE WOULD LIKE TO EXPRESS a special thanks to those who helped this project along. First, we are grateful to Dan Treier, who provided both of us with the opportunity to explore the doctrine of the priesthood of all believers during our doctoral studies. We appreciate also our LA "Inklings" group that read and commented on chapters of this book. Your care and insights have benefited this project. We are grateful for David Congdon and the IVP staff who saw this project from proposal to completion. Hank would like to thank Dr. Don Davis and the staff at The Urban Ministry Institute for their encouragement and their deep commitment to fleshing out the doctrine of the priesthood of all believers. Uche would like to thank Biola University for providing a research and development grant, which lightened his teaching load and freed him to work on this project. Thanks also to Chad Duarte for cheerfully compiling the index. Finally, thank you to Johanna and Melissa who faithfully encouraged us (and continue to do so) along the way.

Portions of chapters two and three contain revised material from Uche's former work, *Kings and Priests: Scripture's Theological Account of Its Readers* (Pickwick, 2014). Portions of chapters four and five contain revised material from Hank's work *The Priesthood of All Believers and the Missio Dei* (Pickwick, 2016). These portions are used by permission of Wipf and Stock Publishers.

1

EXALTED CLERGY OR EGALITARIAN PRIESTS?

*For through him [Christ] we both have
access in one Spirit to the Father.*

EPHESIANS 2:18

✆

DEVELOPING A FAITHFUL DOCTRINE of the church is a practical and theological challenge facing the global evangelical church in the twenty-first century. Pastors and church leaders are asking new questions about the church and often finding the answers of previous generations unsatisfactory. One Roman Catholic author suggests that "as far as the development of doctrine is concerned, the twentieth century was the century of the church."[1] We believe something similar may be said at the end of this century—if the Lord tarries—about the Protestant and indigenous churches exploding around the globe. In the midst of rapid change, a return to the sources can provide much-needed guidance for a new generation of missional disciples. Some five hundred years ago, similar winds of change were blowing. At that time the doctrine of the priesthood of all believers was retrieved by a man named Martin Luther. The doctrine became a pillar for the Protestant church and continues to possess powerful resources for the church today. Yet like any good thing—money, sex or power, for example—the doctrine of the priesthood of all believers can be used for good or ill. What is a faithful and fruitful understanding of the doctrine of the priesthood of all believers?

POTENTIAL PRIESTHOOD PROBLEMS

Ordained priests have recently received much negative attention. Headlines abound: "Priest Faces 7 Years for Endangering Children," "Archbishop, Under Fire over Abuse, Apologizes but Says He Won't Resign," "U.N. Panel Says Vatican Is Lax over Abusive Priests" and so on.[2] In much of Europe and North America ordained priesthood is associated in the popular imagination with scandal, cover-ups and abuses of power. Others find themselves confused and ambivalent regarding clergy, describing priests as at once holy, detached, committed, aloof, devoted and out of touch.

At one end of the spectrum, there is the admirable Bishop Myriel of *Les Miserables*—a paragon of goodness and mercy. The novel begins with a description of Myriel's characteristic benevolence. When he arrives in Digne he is installed in the episcopal palace, "a vast and handsome town house built in stone," which happens to be next to a hospital. Three days after his arrival the bishop visits the hospital, and upon seeing its small size and bad conditions he resolves to house its twenty-six poor patients in his palace and himself in the hospital.[3] It is this same priest who later welcomes the vagrant Jean Valjean with open arms. Who can forget the scene where, after running off in the night with the bishop's silverware, Valjean is apprehended by police and escorted back to Myriel? When the police inform the priest that they found his silver in the thief's bag, the priest responds by turning to Valjean and saying, "Ah, there you are. Am I glad to see you! But, heavens! I gave you the candlesticks, too, you know; they are made of silver like the rest and you can get two hundred francs for them, easily. Why didn't you take them with the cutlery?" Upon giving the crook the candlesticks, he releases him and sends him on his way to go and become "an honest man."[4]

At the other end of the spectrum, one might think (scornfully) of Jane Austen's fairly irreligious parson, Rev. Collins, whose high esteem of himself and his authority as clergy "made him altogether a mixture of pride and obsequiousness, self-importance and humility."[5]

Yet for many of the faithful the ordained priest stands at the top of an ecclesiastical hierarchy—one, perhaps, divinely instituted—as a go-between for God and his people. When the ordained priest comes to be seen as categorically different from and highly elevated above the common believer, it is no wonder that falls from grace amount to catastrophes.

What about the "priesthood of *all believers*"? What comes to mind when this notion is trumpeted? If we entertain some of the previously mentioned concepts of priesthood, it is difficult to imagine anything good coming from the idea. One reaction might be a sense of incongruence between what is being affirmed ("Everyone's a priest to God!") and our honest self-evaluation ("Me, a priest?!"). The syllogism is simple: (1) If priests are holy (or anything else we typically ascribe to priests) and (2) we are not, then (3) we are not priests. For those with such a mindset, the priesthood of all believers is not a doctrine so readily embraced. That's the first potential problem.

Second, the doctrine has often come to mean something akin to the First Amendment right to "freedom of speech" or "to

petition the [church] Government for a redress of grievances."
Under the guise of freedom of conscience or religious liberty
(two wonderful concepts, mind you), the priesthood of believers has sometimes been used to sanction unfettered individualism and schism in Christ's church. If I do not approve of
another's judgment, I can simply secede and band together with
those who agree with me. According to one story, likely satirical,
a Georgia church split forty-eight times in a hundred-year
period.[6] Denominations, factions and sects often appear to be
the natural offspring of the priesthood of all believers.

We are thus confronted with two potential priesthood
problems: clerical priesthood and individualistic priesthood. The
former sometimes manifests itself in unhealthy hierarchy, the
latter in unfettered democracy—and neither is desirable. What,
then, do we mean when we declare every Christian a priest? Is
the priesthood of all believers a concept worth salvaging?

A COMMON PRIESTHOOD?

Yes! The doctrine of the priesthood of all believers is essential for
the church today! However, as with many doctrines, the devil is in
the details. Much depends on how we understand and practice the
doctrine. Ordained leadership need not carry with it the aura of
superiority, and believers' priesthood need not be individualistic.
Both official leadership and the priesthood of all believers are necessary for Christ's body to grow into maturity (see Eph 4:11-16).

When we look at the New Testament, we discover that no
ordained Christian leader is explicitly called "priest."[7] This term
is reserved for Christ and for all of God's people. During the first
two centuries of the post-apostolic church, priestly language and
imagery were similarly applied in this restricted manner.[8] Justin
Martyr (AD 100–165), for example, identifies Christians as a

priestly race because of their unique election, unique worship and unique mission (i.e., preaching for the conversion of humankind).[9] Being a priest is at the core of what it means to be a Christian. It is an identity, not simply a set of lofty but optional tasks one might perform should he or she choose. Priesthood connotes a dignity before God and a responsibility to creation. That such a motley crew as the church should be given such a designation seems completely out of touch with reality. Nevertheless it is true, and therefore must be regularly restated.

Early church theologians such as the author of the *Didache*, Tertullian (d. AD 222) and Origen (d. AD 254) would sometimes describe church leaders as priests, but they never did so in a way that denied the priesthood of all believers. Origen's sermons on Leviticus, for instance, regularly appeal to the "royal priesthood" described in 1 Peter 2:9. He speaks of believers as a "spiritual priesthood" and applies priesthood to all believers at least a dozen times.[10] Origen's example illustrates that, for the most part, the title "priest" applied to all believers during the early centuries of the church.[11] This emphasis on the priesthood of all believers never completely faded from the church's consciousness, but it did undergo a decline—what we might call "the dark ages" of the doctrine (the medieval period)—until its rehabilitation by Luther and others (described in some detail in chapter three). Today the doctrine goes by different names within different traditions: "the priesthood of the baptized" (most often used in the Orthodox communion), "the priesthood of the faithful" (the preferred term among Roman Catholics) and "the priesthood of all believers" (usually used by Protestants and global indigenous church movements). Each term, carrying slightly different connotations, can helpfully illumine an important aspect of the doctrine, and we will look at each in turn.

The priesthood of the baptized (Orthodox). One writer observes that "the Orthodox baptismal rite preserves to this day the idea of the ordination of the laics."[12] Another writer notes that the connection between baptism and ordination into the universal priesthood is "found uniformly in Latin, Greek and Syriac writers of the early Church."[13] Contemporary Orthodox theologian John Zizioulas writes, "It must be said emphatically, that there is no such thing as 'non-ordained' persons in the Church." He elaborates on the connection between baptism and ordination:

> Baptism and especially confirmation as an inseparable aspect of the mystery of Christian initiation involves a "laying on of hands." . . . The East has kept these two aspects (baptism—confirmation) not only inseparably linked with one another but also with what follows, namely *the eucharist*. The theological significance of this lies in the fact that *it reveals the nature of baptism and confirmation as being essentially an ordination*. . . . The immediate and inevitable result of baptism and confirmation was that the newly baptized would *take his particular "place" in the eucharistic assembly*, i.e. *that he would become a layman*. That this implies ordination is clear from the fact that the baptized person does not simply become a "Christian," as we tend to think, but he becomes a *member of a particular "ordo"* [structure] in the eucharistic community.[14]

For the Orthodox Church baptism does not merely initiate someone into the church, but it gives them a particular office; namely, a priestly layperson—one who participates in the church's worship (chiefly the Eucharist) in a particular way. To be a Christian is to be simultaneously baptized and ordained for a certain kind of priestly ministry. Hence the preferred Orthodox term for the doctrine is the "priesthood of the baptized."[15]

The priesthood of the faithful (Roman Catholic). The Second Vatican Council's *Lumen Gentium* is the first conciliar document to address "the common priesthood of the faithful."[16] It provides a clear affirmation that the whole church is a priestly people—in a manner reminiscent of Luther and other Protestants. Archbishop Oscar Romero explained the teaching of the Roman Catholic Church to his parishioners this way:

> How beautiful will be the day when all the baptized under-
> stand that their work, their job, is a priestly work, . . . and
> each metalworker, each professional, each doctor with the
> scalpel, the market woman at her stand, is performing a
> priestly office! How many cabdrivers, I know, listen to this
> message there in their cabs; you are a priest at the wheel,
> my friend, if you work with honesty, consecrating that taxi
> of yours to God, bearing a message of peace and love to the
> passengers who ride in your cab.[17]

Roman Catholic doctrine teaches that there is only one priesthood—Christ's—but there are two distinct participations in it—one ministerial, belonging to ordained clergy, the other common, belonging to all baptized believers. Christ the high priest made the church into a kingdom and priests to serve God. The Catholic catechism reads: "Through the sacraments of Baptism and Confirmation the faithful are 'consecrated to be . . . a holy priesthood,'" and they live out their baptismal priesthood "through their participation, each according to his own vocation, in Christ's mission as priest, prophet, and king."[18] Each Christian exercises his or her priesthood in a distinctive way, in accordance with their calling. Within the baptismal priesthood of the faithful, a subgroup is ordained to the ministerial priesthood. This group of ordained leaders are the ones most people think about when the word *priest* is mentioned. They lead congregations in celebrations of the Lord's Supper, preach the Word of God, baptize and perform other duties in the Roman Catholic Church. For Catholics the ordained priesthood is special, with a unique sacrament, but it exists to serve the common priesthood. It is "the means by which Christ unceasingly builds up and leads his Church."[19] While "the common priesthood of the faithful" is the most common term used by Roman Catholic theologians, many now also use the traditionally Protestant "priesthood of all believers."[20]

The priesthood of all believers (Protestant). Martin Luther did not coin the phrase "the priesthood of all believers"—the closest he comes is the "general priesthood of all baptized believers"—but he remains the most important source for the Protestant understanding of the doctrine, referring to believers as priests hundreds of times throughout his writings. The doctrine, according to Luther, denotes the believer's sharing in Christ's royal priesthood through faith and baptism. Its primary implications are every believer's access to the Father through Christ and responsibility to minister to other believers, especially through the proclamation of the Word.

Other traditions took up Luther's mantle, some conforming to his intent and others diverging. For example, the Anabaptist traditions held what Luther deemed a radicalized version of the doctrine. Like Luther, they emphasized believers' direct access to God, although they sometimes minimized the role of ordained leaders in the church. One writer observes:

> The experience of the immediacy with God led Anabaptists to reject any notion that special places, persons or objects

brought one closer to God. The relationship of the human being with God was not dependent on clerical or sacramental mediation. In the Anabaptist view, religious institutions were human inventions, at best, and downright detrimental to spiritual well being at worst. . . . The spiritual experience of the immediate relationship between God and human beings had the consequence of elevating the common person to a position equal to that of the clergy and nobility.[21]

In addition to this emphasis, Anabaptists stressed the responsibility of every believer to preach the gospel to those without a sincere faith in Christ. This missional dimension of the priesthood of all believers "contributed greatly to the launching of the modern missionary movement . . . a logical result of a church-view which made every baptized person a missioner."[22] While different Protestant traditions have emphasized different aspects of the doctrine, a common core can be identified.

The heart of the Protestant understanding of the priesthood of believers is Trinitarian. First, the baptized believer now has direct access to the Father in the Most Holy Place. Through Christ we can all experience God intimately. Second, as those who have been united to Christ we have the privilege of priestly ministry to one another in the place of Christ, especially as we speak his words and announce the good news about his grace and forgiveness. Finally, every member of the priesthood of all believers has received the Holy Spirit's anointing and empowerment for mission and witness in the world. Each baptized believer has received gifts for service and ministry. Just as Jesus was empowered for mission at his baptism, so baptized believers have received the Holy Spirit's empowerment. They too are now called to join in the *missio Dei*—the mission of God in the world.

The principles and practices of the priesthood of all believers must be considered carefully lest the doctrine become a wax nose twisted in unseemly directions. How we finish the statement "We believe in the priesthood of all believers, therefore . . ." reveals a good deal about what *we* understand the doctrine to mean. At my (Uche's) church, for example, the sentence might be completed with any of the following statements:

- We share the preaching responsibilities among a group of five to ten teachers.
- We place much of the directing of the church in the hands of laypeople.
- We speak of small group leaders as the "real" pastors of the church.
- We treat small groups as the heartbeat of the church, the place where all members are encouraged to "speak the truth in love" to one another.
- We devote large portions of our service times to hearing spontaneous prayers and words of testimony from various members of the congregation.
- We have reflection services where the congregation "preaches the sermon" through spontaneous reflections on Scripture.

Without evaluating the relative strengths or weaknesses of these practices, we can see that they betray a *particular* take (a fairly Anabaptistic one) on what the priesthood of all believers entails. In fact, all renderings of the doctrine are contextual and their validity rests on how much they cohere with Scripture's overall vision. As will become clear, some practices necessarily follow from an affirmation of the priesthood of believers and some do not.

Despite their differences, the above terms—"priesthood of the faithful," "priesthood of the baptized" and "priesthood of all believers"—all faithfully express aspects of Scripture's teaching. Also of significance is the fact that all major traditions of the church emphasize this doctrine as vitally important for local congregations today.

A THEOLOGICAL VISION FOR THE DOCTRINE

The priesthood of all believers lies near the center of church life and Christian spirituality. Rather than simply being a quaint Protestant slogan, it is a way of naming the Christian's identity in Jesus Christ. As with many other teachings, fresh restatements must be made so that its truth remains living in the consciousness of the church. This book is one such contemporary restatement. We aim to present a well-rounded theological vision for the priesthood of all believers, one that is constructive rather than reactive. It develops in four stages— biblical, historical, theological and practical—with a chapter devoted to each stage.

The *biblical* chapter (chapter two) outlines the story of the priesthood of all believers. It is a story that begins in Eden and ends in the New Jerusalem, but we focus on a few highlights, starting with Exodus 19:4-6 followed by Psalm 110 and Isaiah 52–66. We then take up 1 Peter 2:4-9 as a programmatic New Testament text, and further build on its insights through an examination of several Pauline writings, Hebrews and the book of Revelation. The chapter also identifies some specific features of the Levitical priesthood, ultimately seeking to highlight the similarities between the labors of professional priests in the Old Testament and those of members of Christ's royal priesthood. Finally, we point to the centrality of the Messiah as the one who fulfills the long-awaited office of eschatological royal priest and initiates the participation of God's people in his own royal priesthood. Through the interweaving of these strands, we have the *beginnings* of a more thorough understanding of what the priesthood of believers entails for the church.

The third chapter is *historical*, detailing Martin Luther's theology of the priesthood of believers and presenting it as a fruitful and concrete attempt to integrate and develop Scripture's teaching on priesthood—both ordained and universal. We place Luther's doctrine in context by setting it against the backdrop of medieval developments in the understanding of priesthood, particularly the elevation of ordained leadership over the laity. Much of Luther's polemic is targeted toward these (negative) shifts. He argues that all believers share the privilege of royal priesthood and are called to "proclaim" the Word in its written, oral and sacramental forms. This chapter serves to correct some misconceptions of Luther's teaching on the matter, while presenting him as a bridge between the biblical material and the present life and thought of the church. Luther's life and teaching illustrate how revitalizing a vision of the priesthood of all believers opens the way for greater transformation of the church's life and mission by the Word of God.

Chapter four is *theological*, arguing that a Christian doctrine of the priesthood of all believers should be developed with a Christocentric-Trinitarian understanding of the *missio Dei*. It brings the doctrine into dialogue with the church's confession of the triune God, producing an explicitly Trinitarian account of the priesthood of believers. We contend that there are especially appropriate ways for the royal priesthood to relate to the Father (worship), the Son (service) and the Holy Spirit (witness). Inadequate Trinitarian versions of the doctrine of the priesthood of all believers can be found in Islam, Mormonism and a number of Protestant theologies. This chapter concludes with a brief critique of several inadequate Protestant forms.

The final substantive chapter is *practical*, providing a contemporary ethics in outline for the royal priesthood. We hold that a canonically and catholically informed notion of the priesthood of all believers leads to particular contextualized ecclesial practices. The chapter addresses how a clear *vision*, a resolute *intention* and particular *means* (VIM) can lead to faithful and fruitful practices. It places particular weight on seven central practices essential to the health of the royal priesthood. These practices are closely associated with those emerging from the earlier chapter on Luther: (1) baptism as public ordination to the royal priesthood, (2) prayer, (3) *lectio divina*, (4) ministry, (5) church discipline, (6) proclamation and (7) the Lord's Supper. Each of these is rooted in the apostolic doctrine of the royal priesthood, and each has played an important role in the doctrine's history. Our hope for this book is that the richness of this doctrine, with its deep biblical and historical roots, will become evident so that its ramifications might be felt in our practices and everyday experience as followers of the great High Priest.

A Brief Note on Authorship

As with many dual-authored books, questions about which author is speaking may arise. While we both share responsibility for the entire book, it may be helpful for the reader to know that chapters one, two and three are primarily authored by Uche, while chapters four, five and six are primarily authored by Hank. Personal illustrations and anecdotes in the respective chapters belong to the primary author of the chapter.

2

A ROYAL PRIESTHOOD

Scripture's Story

The LORD has sworn
and will not change his mind,
"You are a priest forever
after the order of Melchizedek."

PSALM 110:4

Although the whole earth is mine, you will
be for me a kingdom of priests.

EXODUS 19:5-6 NIV

A T FIRST GLANCE IT MIGHT APPEAR that the doctrine of the priesthood of all believers has a slender biblical basis comprising a handful of scriptural passages: 1 Peter 2:4-9, Revelation 1:6 and Revelation 5:10. Not only that, but some scholarship denies that the concept can be found anywhere in these verses or in the entire New Testament. John Elliott, for instance, writes in the introduction to his monograph-length treatment of 1 Peter 2:4-10, "The relatively few references to the 'universal priesthood of all believers' in this study indicate that this theme, though the original stimulus of this investigation, proved insignificant, if not altogether useless, in the specific exegesis of the text."[1] It would be unwise, however, to stop with first glances, as those can often be misleading. When examined more closely Scripture offers a bounty of material that goes toward funding a robust doctrine of the priesthood of all believers. The aim of this chapter is to bring out some of those riches—first by outlining the Old and New Testaments' teaching on the priesthood of believers, highlighting Genesis 1–2, Exodus 19:4-6 and 1 Peter 2:4-9 as the programmatic texts, as well as Isaiah 56–66, the Pauline corpus and the books of Hebrews and Revelation. Second, the chapter identifies some specific features of the Israelite priesthood, ultimately seeking to fill out a picture of the universal priesthood through an examination of the particular labors or ministries of professional priests. Finally, we draw attention to Scripture's depiction of Christ as the one who fulfills the office of priest and invites his church to participate in his priesthood. Through the interweaving of these three strands, we will have the *beginnings* of a more thorough understanding of the priesthood of believers and what this priesthood might entail for the church. Contrary to Elliott, who concludes that "the New Testament contains no unanimous viewpoint on the subject of Christian priesthood,"[2] we will see that the Bible is rich, multifaceted and unified in its portrait of the priesthood of all believers.

ROYAL PRIESTHOOD IN THE GARDEN SANCTUARY: ADAM THE PRIEST-KING

Adam as king. The story of the royal priesthood truly begins at the very beginning. In the book of Genesis, both Adam and

Melchizedek are portrayed as priest-kings. We will return to Melchizedek later; for now we start with Genesis 1. Here we see that human beings are the crown of God's creation. Although the precise meaning of the two terms is a contentious issue, the idea of humanity as the "image" and "likeness" of God in Genesis 1:26-27 presents one avenue toward grasping what human beings are meant to be.[3] Two things are noteworthy for our discussion. First, the creation of humanity in the image of God is tied to their unique relation to God. Second, image is connected to the exercise of authority over the nonhuman creation. The association of *image* with humanity's rulership over the nonhuman world is confirmed in both 1:26 and 1:28. The term *rule* is often tied in the Old Testament to kingship or the rule of political leaders (Ps 72:8; 110:2; Is 14:6; Ezek 34:4).[4] In Genesis 1, what is a political term is applied to the dominion of humans over the created order.[5] The verb translated as "subdue" furthermore refers to bringing something or someone under subjection by the exercise of power. In Genesis 1:28 the term then expresses humanity's responsibility and privilege to spread throughout the earth and make it a habitable home. Both terms taken together connote humankind's royal status and duty of ruling over the entire nonhuman creation—plants and animals alike. Indeed, a central purpose for humanity being created in the image of God is that men and women would exercise royal rule.[6] D. J. A. Clines says it well: "Though man's rulership over the animals is not itself the image of God, no definition of the image is complete which does not refer to this function of rulership."[7] Whatever "image of God" denotes is inextricably tied to the subduing of and ruling over the earth as royalty before God.[8] Humanity is *representational* and *representative*, being like God in the exercise of rule over the earth while receiving delegated authority.[9] There is both royal dignity and responsibility in the *imago Dei*.[10]

Adam as priest. The focus of our study is on the sacral dimension of humanity's role on the earth. A number of scholars see many similarities between the Garden of Eden in Genesis 2–3 and the tabernacle and temple in Israel.[11] G. K. Beale, for example, presents at least fourteen signs that Israel's later tabernacle and temple are to be seen as recapitulations and reflections of God's first temple, Eden.[12] One of the signs, and for our purposes the most important one, is that the garden is the place of the first priest. Beale argues, first, that the two Hebrew words often rendered as "cultivate and keep" in Genesis 2:15 are usually translated "serve and guard" elsewhere in the Old Testament, and when they occur together they refer either to Israelites serving God and keeping his word or to priests keeping the service of the tabernacle (Num 3:7-8; 8:25-26; 18:5-6; 1 Chron 23:32; Ezek 44:14).[13] Second, Beale points to a number of ancient Jewish sources that describe Adam in priestly ways.[14] Gordon Wenham further notes that the clothing of Adam in tunics of skin parallels the accounts of priestly ordination wherein Moses clothes Aaron and his sons in tunics (Ex 28:41; 29:8; 40:14; Lev 8:13).[15] In light of these observations as well as the pervasive sanctuary imagery in Genesis 2–3 it would appear that Adam is portrayed, against the later picture of the Israelite priesthood and temple, as the "archetypal priest" who served in God's primal temple.[16] Thus, taken together with our prior discussion of humankind's kingship, Adam is both king and priest—a royal priest, as it were. This theme of Adam as priest-king was also emphasized among various early Christian theologians.[17]

In Genesis 2:15, after the creation of the first man, Yahweh takes Adam and places him in the garden *to serve* and *guard it*, herein outlining some of his priestly duties. Viewing the garden as a temple allows for the multivalence of the two words. Adam, on the one hand, is to be a gardener who quite literally tends the garden and maintains its order. Yet on the other hand, his work is to serve God in the garden and guard the arboreal sanctuary from uncleanness and intruders.[18] This spade work—this *vocation*—in the garden is priestly work. Then in the form of a twofold command God further defines how this priestly task is to be understood. The man is first *permitted* to partake to his heart's delight of anything in the garden. He is however *prohibited* from eating of the tree of the knowledge of good and evil, on penalty of death (Gen 2:16-17).[19] Adam is to conduct his work within the liberating confines of the word of Yahweh so that the order of the garden might not be disrupted. The command of God undoubtedly shapes Adam's understanding of his priestly duties, impressing on him that his labor is not outside the rule of God but rather is either fortified or frustrated based on his response to God's word. Walter Brueggemann notes that it is the three key aspects in this account—vocation, permission and prohibition—that characterize human beings. The chief human task is to find a way to hold the three together and thus fulfill the role of royal priest by keeping Yahweh's sovereign word.[20]

Perhaps a way to unify the functions of tending the garden and attending to God's word might be to see them as one act of *expanding the sanctuary of God*.[21] As those created in the image of the divine King, humanity was to spread and reflect his glorious reign by subduing and ruling the entire earth (Gen 1:26-28). Beale draws attention to Babylonian and Egyptian traditions that present humans as created to serve their god in a temple and to extend that god's fame by building more temples or widening the parameters of an original temple.[22] Moreover, images of the gods were customarily placed in the temples. Thus Adam as both king-priest and image of God was placed in the garden sanctuary with the task of expanding its boundaries. In this light, the commission to cultivate/serve and guard/keep the garden (Gen 2:15) is probably part of the commission to subdue and rule the earth as royal priests (Gen 1:26-28).[23] Beale summarizes the point well: "They were on the primeval hillock of hospitable Eden, outside of which lay the inhospitable land. They were to extend the smaller liveable area of the garden by transforming the outer chaotic region into a habitable territory."[24] To subdue the earth was to extend God's garden sanctuary throughout the earth and thus prepare the way for the presence of Yahweh to permeate the world in its entirety. This end would be achieved by obedience to God's commands and the publication of the same throughout the earth and to succeeding generations.[25]

THE FOUNDING OF A PRIESTLY PEOPLE: EXODUS

"A kingdom of priests." God's program to found a priestly people continues in Israel's deliverance from Egypt as recounted in the book of Exodus. After the Lord rescues his people from Egypt's army (Ex 14), miraculously provides food and water (Ex 15:22-27; 16:1-21; 17:1-7) and secures the defeat of the Amalekites (Ex 17:8-16), the people arrive at Mount Sinai (Ex 19:1-2), where Moses is to ascend the mountain to meet with God on behalf of the people (Ex 19:3). The Lord speaks to him, beginning with a reminder of God's past dealings with Israel: the plagues on Egypt, how he bore them "on eagles' wings" and brought them to himself (Ex 19:4). By the use of three "I" statements ("what *I* did to the Egyptians," "*I* bore you on eagles' wings," "*I* brought you to myself"), this early episode calls attention to the fact that the privilege and calling of royal priesthood (which will be brought out in the next verses) is not something procured by one's desiring, but finds its root in divine initiative. God establishes the priesthood; we do not.

Then come the crucial verses. Here we find a proclamation of God's favor followed by a call to covenantal obedience: "If you will indeed obey my voice . . . you shall be to me a kingdom of priests" (Ex 19:5-6). This conditional promise does not suggest that Israel must earn their status as a royal priests, but that they will live out their status by fulfilling their end of the bargain. John Davies observes: "The emphasis on this reading falls on the divine initiative, not on a *quid-pro-quo* arrangement. The relationship already exists and is the basis for the appeal for (continued) loyalty."[26] Should they keep the covenant by obeying God's voice, they will *continue* to be a special, covenant people to the Lord and thus fulfill their calling. Divine favor primarily determines their privileged status.[27] To be God's people is to accept the privileges and responsibilities involved in keeping his covenant.

Three images are used to express the privileges promised to Israel: "treasured possession," "holy nation" and "kingdom of priests." The first two images connote the privileged status of Israel as God's special, set apart and loved possession. Although the whole earth belongs to God, he takes this people for his treasure, his consecrated ones. The third image—the focus of our book—contains similar emphases. Whether rendered as "kings, priests," "kingly priests," "royal priesthood" or "kingdom of priests," this title given to Israel preserves the theme of bestowed honor and dignity granted to God's people.[28] However, how is one to understand the term *priesthood*? How might Moses' hearers or subsequent readers have understood Israel's calling as priests? It seems probable that the less familiar notion of a universal priesthood would have been read in light of what is more familiar—namely, the official priesthood. "The reader of Exodus 19," Davies writes, "is assumed to have knowledge of some form of institutional priesthood (vv. 22, 24). It is difficult to believe, then, that Israelite readers were not to make a conceptual connection between *kōhēn* (priest) in Exod 19.6 and the priesthood of their experience, or with the other occurrences of the word in the same document."[29] If this is true, then another commentator is correct when he writes, "The priest's place and function within society must serve as the ideal model for Israel's self-understanding of its role among the nations. The priest is set apart by a distinctive way of life consecrated to the service of God and dedicated to ministering to the needs of the people."[30] If the official priesthood is the model for understanding Israel's corporate priesthood, then it would be appropriate to reflect on the character and function of the former, as it will shed light on the nature of the latter.

What is a priest, really? The Hebrew term *kōhēn* is used to designate Israelite priests as well as those of Gentile nations (e.g., Gen 41:45; 1 Sam 5:5; 2 Kings 10:19).[31] The use of the term indicates that it speaks of those who mediate between God and the general population. To be called a priest was to be bestowed with an honor on the level of royalty. Priests have the honor of continual access to the presence of the Lord in the sanctuary, but they also bear the responsibilities of offering sacrifices for the people, helping them discern holy from profane and clean from unclean, teaching the law, applying its commands to the varying circumstances of Israel's life and blessing the people in the Lord's name. The rationale for the priesthood is summed up well by Davies:

> If the sanctuary is *bêt yhwh* ("the home of Yhwh," Exod. 23.19), then the priest is at least a regular visitor to that divine abode, a welcome and honoured beneficiary of the divine hospitality. The priest belongs in two worlds. While his everyday life is among his fellow Israelites, when he

dons his vestments and crosses the threshold he becomes a participant in the heavenly or ideal world.[32]

As the Lord's honored guest and servant, the priest is both the model and the provision for Israel's royal priesthood.[33] The term *priest* chiefly designates one who has to do with the word of God.[34] T. F. Torrance brings out the significance of this connection, writing, "All that the priest does, all liturgical action, answers to the Word given to the priest who bears that Word and mediates it to man, and only in relation to that primary function does he have the other functions of oblation and sacrifice."[35] The priest's ministry of the word pertains primarily to his instructing of the people in God's law. However, even the offering of sacrifices is a testimony to God's saving will and an obedient response to the word that initiated the sacrifices, so that every ministry the priest does is somehow a ministry of God's covenantal word.[36] While we rightly think of sacrifice when we think of priests, it is important to highlight several other possibly less obvious, but critical, ministries of the priest—ministries of the word—that will prove helpful in filling out an account of the nature of priesthood and informing the practices of the universal priesthood: discerning between holy and profane, teaching, judging legal matters, public reading and pronouncing blessing.

Discerning. After Yahweh destroys Aaron's two sons for desecrating his altar, he speaks to Aaron and prescribes his primary responsibilities as a priest (Lev 10:8-11). Aaron's first duty is to distinguish between the holy and profane, and the clean and unclean. To be holy is to be set apart for God and separated from the common. If holy things become defiled they must be purged immediately or the community will incur God's judgment. The unclean and the holy should never come together. Priests were to guard holy space (tabernacle, temple), holy time (sabbath, holy days) and the covenant holiness of all of God's people.[37] Holiness was such a serious matter that the Levitical priests were authorized to kill members of the covenant community who flagrantly disregarded their covenant with Yahweh (Ex 32:25-29; Num 18:1-7; 25:1-18; 35:31-34). Thus the first duty of the priest was to preserve the holiness of holy things and minister to the people by properly discerning the distinctions the law requires between these categories of objects.[38]

Teaching. The second responsibility of the priesthood was to instruct Israel in all the statutes that Yahweh had given to Moses (Lev 10:11). In Moses' blessing of the Levites, he pronounces, "They shall teach Jacob your rules and Israel your law" (Deut 33:10). The perpetual mandate for the priesthood of Israel was that they would instruct the people in torah and in that way help to preserve healthy covenantal relations between God and Israel. This is borne out in the prophets, where the priests are sometimes indicted for not fulfilling this very purpose (e.g., Jer 6; 8; Mal 1–2).

Judging. Deuteronomy 17:8-13 prescribes legal protocols in cases too difficult for local authorities to handle, thus requiring the expertise of priests at the sanctuary. Gordon McConville lists, for example, the issues of distinguishing between murder and manslaughter (Ex 21:12-14), pronouncing on the seriousness of an assault or theft (Ex 21:18-21) and deciding when negligence becomes culpable (Ex 21:28-29).[39] As experts in the law, the priests would explain its stipulations to the parties involved and render a verdict. The decision announced by the high priest would be binding on all parties (Deut 17:11-13). Thus pronouncing faithful judgments—applying the law to difficult matters—was to be an ongoing practice of the priesthood that would help keep the people faithful to the Lord even in the details of everyday life.

Reading. In Moses' parting exhortations to the children of Israel (Deut 31:9-13) he commands that every seven years, at the Feast of Booths, the priests are to assemble the people and the law is to be read before all of Israel. The purpose of this communal reading is to instill the fear of the Lord and obedience to his law into every generation. We see this practice carried out after the exile and rebuilding of Jerusalem's wall, when Ezra reads and interprets the law before the people of Israel (Neh 8). Ezra and all priests function as those who are responsible for weaving the law into the fabric of Israel's worship life in perpetuity, so that those "who have not known" (Deut 31:13) will no longer be ignorant.

Blessing. A final role of priests was to pronounce blessing on Israel: "At that time the LORD set apart the tribe of Levi to carry the ark of the covenant of the LORD to stand before the LORD to minister to him *and to bless in his name,* to this day" (Deut 10:8; cf. 21:5). Numbers 6:22-27 presents this priestly blessing in its paradigmatic form, for not only does the passage command the recitation of a blessing but it also prescribes the shape the blessing should take.[40] The blessing itself is found in verses 24-26, where each verse contains one or two specific petitions or promises:

> The LORD bless you and keep you;
> the LORD make his face to shine upon you and be
>   gracious to you;
> the LORD lift up his countenance upon you and give you
>   peace.

The blessing is not some kind of incantation or even a typical prayer, but rather something in between. It is a pronouncement directed toward the people (note the repeated use of *you*) by the priest, but that, through the threefold use of the name of

Yahweh, emphasizes that it is God who is the source of blessing, not the priest. When the same blessing is voiced over and over again in changing times and circumstances, it functions as a pronouncement of God's will and promise to bless his covenant people continually, particularly as they walk faithfully before him. As one commentator puts it, the blessing, in different ways, "gives expression to God's commitment to Israel—a commitment which promises earthly security, prosperity, and general well-being."[41] The priest is the mediator of God's promise of providential care.

The common feature of all these ministries is their clear public and word-centered orientation. Priests bring the word of the Lord to bear on the entirety of Israel's existence, in the everyday and sacred dimensions as well as the legal and cultic. Priests were the heralds of the will of Yahweh, especially as they interpreted the word for the people and applied it to the difficult and various circumstances of Israel's community life. These priestly practices contributed in different ways to forming a covenantally faithful people by constantly directing the gaze of the community to the very covenantal word that formed it.

Professional priests and the royal priesthood. In light of the above, it is clear that Israel's vocation as priests has both vertical and horizontal dimensions. On the one hand, the people were consecrated by the Lord and called to remain set apart from the surrounding nations by obeying Yahweh's gracious commands. On the other hand, each member of the community is responsible for the collective holiness of the people and of the nations. As the epithets "treasured possession" and "holy nation" stress election and the call to holiness and obedience, so "kingdom of priests" or "royal priesthood" emphasizes Israel's unique relationship to God and consequent responsibility to be holy, not only before him but *for* the community and the world. God's people are to function as priests in a manner similar to the professional priesthood. In fact, the special priesthood of Aaron and the Levites is supportive of Israel's corporate priesthood, providing both the model and the means for its preservation. In the end, then, initiation into royal priesthood, like initiation into the Levitical priesthood, is initiation into a particular type of relationship with God, his Word, his people and his world.

ROYAL PRIESTHOOD ROOTED IN DAVID'S SON: PSALM 110

The first time the word *priest* appears in the canon it describes Melchizedek, the original priest-king of Jerusalem. Melchizedek is next mentioned in Psalm 110, where the Lord swears to David's greater Son, "You are a priest forever after the order of Melchizedek" (Ps 110:4). This text and its surrounding verses was arguably the most important Scripture for the royal priesthood in the first century AD, as it is alluded to or cited as many as thirty-three times in the New Testament.[42] The psalm also played a central role in how Jesus conceived of his own mission, culminating in his royal and priestly self-offering on the cross. In this light, it is important that we pause for a moment and reflect on this most important psalm and its contribution to a doctrine of royal priesthood.

The psalm begins with an utterance from Yahweh to his appointed king: "Sit at my right hand, until I make your enemies your footstool" (Ps 110:1). The utterance is heightened by a parallel oath in verse 4: "You are a priest forever after the order [or after the manner] of Melchizedek."[43] This type of an oath is found elsewhere in the psalms associated with the Davidic covenant (Ps 89:3-4, 34-36).[44] These parallel statements from the mouth of

Yahweh strikingly declare that the one who is to be king will also be an everlasting priest! This priesthood, just like the kingship, will not have a train of successors, nor will it be superseded.[45] Rather, as one not in the order of Aaron or Levi but in the order of Melchizedek, the Davidic Son will have a permanent, perpetual office of mediating between God and his covenant people. This notion of a royal priest is carried forward and extended in Isaiah's portrait of the Servant, who not only will be a king-priest but will restore royal priesthood to God's people.

RESTORATION THROUGH THE PRIESTLY SERVANT: ISAIAH 52–66

Israel's vocation as a royal priesthood was by and large left unfulfilled throughout much of its history. If they were to fulfill their calling, it would require intervention of an eschatological sort. Indeed, this is what we find promised in the latter part of the book of Isaiah. Here we discover the promise of a royal priestly "Servant" who will restore his seed, God's people, to their rightful status and service. Let's first take a brief look at the priestly Servant, as this will help establish the main features of the life and ministry of his seed.

The Servant (Isaiah 52–53). Although there is certainly some debate regarding the nature and work of the Servant in Isaiah, many writers now recognize him as a royal priestly figure who performs a priestly ministry.[46] Previous figures who received the designation "my servant" include the likes of Moses and David, both of whom had royal dignity and performed priestly work. In Isaiah 52–53 there are several indications that the Servant is a priest. First, he sprinkles many nations (Is 52:15), as former priests sprinkled water and blood over the people as a form of cleansing. Second, he offers himself as a sacrificial lamb on behalf of the sins of the people so that many will be made righteous (Is 53:7, 10-11). Finally, the Servant performs the priestly task of making "intercession for the transgressors" (53:12), coming before God on behalf of a sinful people. Although other dimensions of the Servant's work could be highlighted, it is fair to say that he is a priestly minister in service of Yahweh and his covenant people. It is this particular calling that will be transferred, so to speak, to his offspring.

The seed (Isaiah 54–66). As mentioned earlier, the restoration of God's people to their priestly vocation is an eschatological reality initiated by the Servant. In this section of Isaiah we find at least four references to the royal priestly office of the restored people (Is 56:1-8; 59:21–60:3; 61; 66:18-21). We will focus on Isaiah 61 (with brief mention of Is 59 and 66) as the most important and explicit treatment of corporate priesthood in the book.[47]

Isaiah 61:6, the clearest intertextual reference to Exodus 19:6 in the Old Testament, is found within a section that focuses on the restoration of Israel and develops the theme of Israel's royal priesthood. Much of the imagery used to portray Israel's restoration is royal and priestly (cf. Is 59:17; 60:16, 21; 61:10; 62:3, 12), but the most explicit priestly reference is found in 61:6. After speaking of the ministry of the anointed Servant (61:1-3) and promising the servitude of foreigners (61:5), Isaiah 61:6 declares: "But you shall be called priests of the LORD; they shall speak of you as the ministers of our God." By contrasting the subjection of "strangers" with the promise of priesthood, Yahweh says in effect, "They will serve you, *but you* will serve *me*." Israel will be clothed in priestly garments (61:3) and render service primarily to Yahweh. It is also the case that this service to God will have a horizontal dimension. The purpose of the nations' marveling at Yahweh's favor toward his people (61:9) is that they would stream to Zion to worship him (cf. Is 2:2). As a priesthood, Israel was to mediate God's blessings to the nations by assisting them in the proper worship of Yahweh and by teaching his ways.[48] This priestly understanding of Israel's vocation is expressed throughout Isaiah, even as early as chapter 2. John Oswalt observes,

> The nations have come, and will come, to Israel . . . to give themselves to the God who is revealed through Israel's experience and through the revelation that has been given to Israel. Whenever "Israel" fails to fulfill its priesthood, failing to make it possible for the nations to call Israel's God *our God*, "Israel" has missed its calling and failed to fulfill the function of its servanthood.[49]

Israel will fulfill its vocation by the grace of God and through the work of the Servant Priest.

The surrounding context of the passage (Isaiah 59–61) suggests that the renewed royal priesthood will involve a new relationship to the word of God. Here the Lord promises his Servant that the Spirit and word in him will "not depart out of your mouth, or out of the mouth of your offspring . . . from this time forth and forevermore" (Is 59:21). The Spirit will enable God's servants to bring about justice and righteousness, particularly through the proclaimed and prophetic word.[50] The saying that the word "shall not depart" is an allusion to Joshua 1:8. Its use in this context suggests that the ministry of Moses and Joshua will be continued by the Servant and his offspring. It speaks of the fact that the presence of the word will be a distinguishing characteristic of the Servant and his priestly seed, and that the people will speak the word and meditate on it continually.[51] If, then, the figure in 59:21 is the Anointed of Isaiah 61:1-3 and the offspring of the former are the restored priestly servants of 61:6, then in the same way that the relationship to Yahweh's word is passed on to his children in 59:21, so the ministry of the Anointed is transferred to the "priests" of 61:6.[52] As priestly offspring, Israel will imitate the work of the anointed Servant by loving God's Word, meditating on it, orienting their lives around it and proclaiming it as good news to the poor and oppressed (Is 61:1-3). This may be the primary way the royal priesthood mediates God's blessings to the nations. In fact, Isaiah 66:18-21 echoes these themes, even expanding priestly privilege to include the nations, who will also see the glory of God, declare that glory to the nations and present fellow Gentiles as offerings to the Lord. Indeed, they will be selected as priests and Levites (Is 66:21) mediating blessing to the world. As we turn to the New Testament, this very notion of God's people as a royal priesthood, the priestly seed of the Servant, is powerfully rearticulated.

THE GREAT HIGH PRIEST: CHRIST'S ESCHATOLOGICAL PRIESTHOOD

The restoration of the people of God promised in Isaiah, and the eschatological priesthood that accompanies it, finds its origin in Jesus Christ, the Servant-Priest. The royal priesthood of Christ is the basis and pattern for the priesthood of all believers. Before tackling the bulk of the New Testament's teaching on universal priesthood, let us examine how the Gospels present Jesus' priestly calling at three stages of his earthly ministry: starting with his baptism, moving to some episodes in the middle (his public ministry) and highlighting a few scenes from his final days.

 The beginning: Baptism. When John the Baptist invited Israel to receive his baptism, he was performing something fairly unique. Rather than the commonplace practice of self-administered baptisms or ceremonial washings, John was performing a priestly act that has as its clearest cognate the washing that takes place during the consecration and ordination of Israel's priests (Ex 29:4; 40:12; Lev 8:6).[53] It appears that John, in baptizing, was ordaining people not into the Levitical priesthood but into an eschatological priesthood. It is in this light that we must view Jesus' baptism. What occurred at Christ's baptism was his initiation into a royal priestly office, being washed, anointed and commissioned for ministry as was the case for Aaronic priests.[54] Moreover, at Jesus' baptism (Mt 3:16-17) the Father endorses his Son with words drawn from two key Scriptures. The first, Psalm 2:7 ("You are my Son . . ."), is a coronation psalm used on occasions when kings would begin their royal service. Its twin passage is Psalm 110, which describes one of David's sons who will be a priest-king like Melchizedek.[55] The second Scripture, Isaiah 42:1 ("Behold my servant . . . in whom my soul delights"), comes at the beginning of a chapter in which God commissions the suffering Servant to his ministry on behalf of Israel—a ministry that ultimately culminates in the sacrificial suffering described in Isaiah 53. Taken together, the use of these passages suggests that Jesus is being depicted as the promised royal priestly Servant. Indeed, in Hebrews 5:5 a quotation of Psalm 2:7 is used to establish Jesus' high priestly ministry. Therefore it is likely that this episode recorded in the Gospels is presenting Jesus as the eschatological Priest-King, who at his baptism is ordained and commissioned for the ministry of restoring Israel and founding a family of royal priests.

The middle: Ministry. The Gospels' portrait of Jesus' earthly ministry also appears to have priestly elements. We will focus on a few episodes in Mark and Luke to illustrate.[56] To begin, a number of passages in the early chapters of Mark's Gospel provide a priestly portrait of Jesus. We will look briefly at four of these. Our first passage, Mark 1:40-45, presents Jesus' healing of a leper. In the Old Testament, the healing ritual and pronouncement were the responsibility of the priests (Lev 13–14). Jesus performs these functions and sends the leper to the official priests to bear witness to his priestly authority.[57] When we read this passage along with Mark 5:25-34, where Jesus heals the woman with a discharge, and Mark 5:35-43, where he raises Jairus's daughter from the dead, we see that Jesus touches and heals people who fit the three conditions for impurity outlined in Numbers 5:1-4. These healing encounters highlight that it is Jesus' holiness, rather than the impurity of others, that is contagious. He reverses the order of impure to pure by transferring his purity to the impure.[58] The connection between this observation and Jesus' priesthood is found in Ezekiel 42:14 and 44:19, two passages that speak of the priest's garments as having the ability to transfer holiness to the people they touch. The people Jesus encounters understand that power flows from his garments (see Mk 6:56).[59] It is likely, therefore, that Mark's depiction of Jesus is a priestly one, since the only biblical precedents for such contagious holiness and power from a garment refer to the priest.

In Mark 2:23-28, Jesus supposedly violates the law by allowing his disciples to pick grain on the sabbath. Three things must be observed here. First, only the priests were allowed to work on the sabbath, since their work was temple work. Second, only priests were permitted to eat the consecrated bread. Third, Jesus and his disciples were not in the temple but in a field. It is possible that what Mark (and Jesus) is conveying is that Jesus as the royal High Priest is himself the location of the sacred space. Therefore his disciples, being bound to him, are given rights as priests to work on the sabbath and as priests are also allowed to eat in that holy place, as David and his men did.[60]

Jesus allows his disciples to do on the sabbath what was by law reserved for the priest, thus implicitly declaring himself and his followers priests.

In another sabbath controversy (Mark 3:1-7), Jesus applies to himself the priestly exemption from sabbath work by healing the man with a shriveled hand. As any good priest should do, Jesus ministers on the sabbath on behalf of the people, indeed working for their benefit.[61] Moreover, through the process of interrogating his opponents Jesus teaches the people the proper interpretation of the law, again showing himself to be a priest.

Finally, Jesus assumes the role of teaching priest in Mark 7:14-23 by offering a fresh interpretation of the laws concerning clean and unclean foods (e.g., Deut 14:4-10). He establishes a new standard by declaring that it is not what enters a person's mouth that makes him unclean but what comes out of it (Mk 7:15). As we have seen, in the Old Testament it was the priest's responsibility to discern for the community what was clean or unclean. Here Jesus takes that charge as the true teacher of Israel.[62] Therefore, although it is not the only image of Jesus in the opening chapters of Mark, the Jesus presented here is certainly a priestly one.[63] For our purposes, we observe that his priestly office is not in these chapters exercised in the form of an atoning sacrifice (as we will see later) but in the functions of healer, purifier and right teacher and interpreter of the law.

Luke's portrayal of a priestly Jesus is perhaps more subtle, but there are some noteworthy elements. First, the priesthood of Jesus is set forth in the early chapters of the Gospel by their emphasis on John the Baptist, whose priestly descent is clearly highlighted. The numerous parallels between John's and Jesus' lives suggest that Luke presents Jesus as John's younger twin.[64] Second, the transfiguration (Lk 9:28-36) signals a priestly Jesus:

James, John and Peter are told to listen to Christ, the teaching Son; the event occurs on the eighth day after Peter's confession, as Aaron began his ministry on the eighth day (Lev 9:1); Jesus' garments are transformed to resemble the glorious robes worn by the high priest; Peter suggests making tents or tabernacles; and Moses and Elijah disappear after the cloud overshadows the mountain (cf. Ex 40:34-38). It is after this event that Jesus resolutely directs his gaze toward Jerusalem, where he will cleanse the temple, teach the people and offer the priestly sacrifice of his own life. The transfiguration proclaims the truth of Jesus' priesthood, just as his baptism did.[65] Finally, in Luke 20:1-8 Jesus is questioned by the chief priests and teachers of the law regarding his authority—his priestly authority in God's house—to cleanse the temple (cf. Lk 19:45-46). Jesus responds in the form of a question concerning John the Baptist's authority, pressing them to pass a (possibly priestly) judgment. Luke is clearly suggesting that Jesus' priestly authority is from God, who gave him the right to cleanse the temple and teach the people.[66] Thus Luke's Gospel presents Jesus as one who is given divine authority to govern the affairs of God's house, primarily through his teaching ministry in and around the temple.

The end: Death. The Gospel writers depict the Last Supper as an enactment of the Servant's role in Isaiah 52–53: Jesus pours out his blood for the forgiveness of sins (Is 53:12; Mt 26:28), he offers himself as the sacrificial lamb and guilt offering (Is 53:10; Mt 26:26; Lk 22:19) and his death will make "many" righteous (Is 53:11; Mt 26:28).[67] Jesus takes on priestly prerogatives—namely, presenting a sacrificial offering, mediating the forgiveness of sins and cleansing people so as to make many righteous. In doing so he declares himself Israel's long-expected Servant-Priest, the agent of God's end-time blessings. Furthermore, the rending of the temple curtain at Jesus' death (Mt 27:51) might be an implicit claim of his priesthood. Following the interpretation provided in Hebrews (e.g., Heb 6:19; 9:3, 8; 10:19-20), some scholars view Jesus' death as that priestly action that makes access to the Holy of Holies possible for all his priestly people.[68] Jesus the high priest removes the barrier between the people of God and the presence of God, forever granting us priestly access through the veil by his blood.

The priestly presentation of Jesus in the Gospels, therefore, takes on a number of dimensions. He is the self-sacrificing priest who offers his body for the sins of the world, but he is also the healer, purifier and teacher of God's law.[69] In all he does, from baptism to his closing prayers (his "high priestly prayer" in Jn 17 and prayer for those crucifying him in Lk 23:34), he stands as the priestly mediator between God and humanity, also setting the pattern for his church to follow.

THE ROYAL PRIESTHOOD OF THE CHURCH: 1 PETER 2

First Peter 2 weaves together three interrelated strands that inform our account of the church's royal priesthood, and all three are found in verses 4 and 5: temple, priesthood and sacrifice. These verses describe Christ as the "living stone" who is rejected by humans (in their rejection of the gospel), but is nevertheless elect and precious to God (1 Pet 2:4). Christians, who are themselves "living stones" by virtue of their connection to the true Living Stone, may find comfort in their suffering because as Christ was vindicated after rejection, so will they be.[70] The living stones metaphor is filled out when believers are referred to as "being built up as a spiritual house," alluding to the temple—our first key strand (1 Pet 2:5).[71] The term *house* may also refer to the people who inhabit or make up the house (e.g., "house of David," "household of faith," "house of Jacob").[72] God's people are a temple people—a clear allusion to priesthood.

The metaphor then shifts from temple to our second important strand: priesthood. The purpose of believers' being built up is that they would be a "holy priesthood" that offers "spiritual sacrifices" acceptable to God through Jesus Christ (1 Pet 2:5). The emphasis of the former phrase is on the communal nature of the priesthood—namely, that believers are a community of priests who, by virtue of God's election in Christ and the sanctifying work of the Spirit, together participate in the benefit of direct access to God.[73] The subject of priestly functions brings us to our third strand: spiritual sacrifices. This phrase highlights the idea that the various sacrifices offered by this priesthood are wrought through the Holy Spirit, making them acceptable to God.[74] One commentator notes that sacrifices consist of "all behavior that flows from a transformation of the human spirit by the sanctifying work of the Holy Spirit (1:2)."[75]

What specifically might these sacrifices include? We would argue that, in light of the broader context of 1 Peter, spiritual sacrifices especially consist of believers' priestly witness in the world in both deed and word. The holy priesthood is to live holy lives before God and the world (1 Pet 3:12), allow their good works to bring glory to God (1 Pet 2:12) and even use wordless good conduct as a means of winning unbelievers to Christ. Even—or especially—within the context of suffering, believers are being formed into a community of sanctified priests whose purpose is to worship God in the Spirit by the performance of sacrificial deeds. However, as we will see, royal priesthood involves proclamation as well.

The other central verse, 1 Peter 2:9, restates but further elaborates on the themes of 2:5—the preciousness, holiness and vocation of

the royal priesthood. The opening phrase ("But you") emphasizes the stark contrast between those who reject Christ and the
church. All four titles originally given to Israel ("chosen race,"
"royal priesthood," "holy nation," "his own possession") are now
applied to the multiethnic church, bringing to mind the gracious
initiative of Yahweh to call and rescue his people. It is important
to note the purpose clause of 1 Peter 2:9: "that you may proclaim
the excellencies of him who called you out of darkness into his
marvelous light." The royal priesthood of believers exists to declare God's *aretas* (Greek: excellencies, virtues, mighty acts,
praises)—a likely reference to Isaiah 43:20-21 (Septuagint),
where those liberated from Babylonian exile would declare the
aretas of God.[76] As both worship *and* evangelism, the Lord's
saved ones proclaim and celebrate the *aretas* of God, particularly his promised and fulfilled redemptive acts.[77] Therefore, as
those brought by new birth into a priestly community, believers
are to walk in holiness and obedience while abounding in good
deeds and announcing the Lord's mighty works. These are the
sacrifices—the acceptable sacrifices—of the royal priesthood.

THE SERVICE OF THE GOSPEL: PAUL'S LETTERS

As we move on from these explicit references to the priesthood
of believers, we come to the implicit teaching of the Pauline
epistles. Here we find that the apostle echoes many of the senti-
ments of the teaching of 1 Peter, while supplementing and filling
them out. We will look briefly at four short passages—two from
Romans and two from Philippians.

Romans. In our first passage, Romans 12:1-2, Paul exhorts believers, in view of God's mercies, to offer their own bodies as living
sacrifices to God. Rather than priests offering slaughtered animals
on an altar, believers are to offer themselves—the entirety of their

being—to God as a sacrifice. Believers are both priests and sacrificial victims, just as Christ is the self-sacrificing high priest.[78] It is notable that it is the task of each Christian to offer his or her body; that is, their priesthood is an individual reality, not merely a corporate one. Royal priesthood is not only the generic call of the church taken as a whole; it is the calling of each member of the body. The focus of these and the subsequent verses is the "temple service" done within the body of Christ, and Paul's language is clearly cultic. Believers' spiritual "worship" or "service" (*latreian*) of offering their bodies as a "sacrifice" is a response to God's saving work. Moreover, the priestly service of believers involves turning from the sinful patterns of the world and being transformed for the purpose of testing and approving the will of God (Rom 12:2). The renewed mind of the believer enables her both to discern and to do what is good and pleasing to God.[79] The offering of ourselves in worship, therefore, is bound up with our moral and spiritual transformation, which itself appears to be wrought by constant exposure and attentiveness to the Word of God.

Speaking of the nature of his own ministry, Paul repeats one of the key themes from 1 Peter 2:4-9—namely, the priestly call to proclaim God's works to the nations. He refers to himself as a "minister" of Jesus Christ "in the priestly service of the gospel," having the goal of presenting the Gentiles as a sacrifice pleasing to God (Rom 15:16). Given the cultic imagery of the passage (e.g., "offering," "acceptable," "sanctified") and the use of the term *priestly*, it is reasonable to see here Paul presented as a priest, who through the success of the gospel presents Gentile converts to God as an acceptable sacrifice.[80] The apostle's ministry is part of the eschatological fulfillment of Isaiah 66:18-20, where the glory of God is declared among the nations and "brothers from all the nations" are presented as an offering to Yahweh.[81] Although

Paul's evangelistic preaching is primarily in view, his priestly service may also extend to his entire ministry of teaching and equipping, which were for the purpose of presenting Christians as mature before God (see Col 1:28). This apostolic ministry of proclaiming the good news, establishing churches and gathering the nations to Christ is the continuing practice and calling of the church. Therefore, all Christians, and particularly those engaged in these enterprises, are priests in service to God.[82]

Philippians. In Philippians 2:17, Paul, suffering for the sake of the gospel, is pictured as a "drink offering" poured out on or alongside the "sacrificial offering" of the Philippians' faith. The image is one of the Levitical priest, whose service involved offering an animal sacrifice accompanied by a drink offering of wine (Num 28:7).[83] Thus the Philippians are portrayed as priests who serve by offering their sacrificial partnership in the gospel, partnership that springs from their faith.[84] Their service of the gospel is accompanied by Paul's sacrificial service—here depicted as a libation—and is as priestly as the apostle's. Like Paul they hold forth the word of life, and in so doing shine like stars in the midst of great darkness (Phil 2:15-16).[85] In this passage priesthood takes place in the midst of suffering, particularly on behalf of the gospel, and involves the giving of oneself wholly for the cause of advancing the good news of God's saving work. In fact, Epaphroditus is called a "minister" in his service to Paul, referring to his ministry in priestly or cultic terms (Phil 2:25). Finally, Philippians 4:18 employs priestly language, speaking of the Philippians' financial gifts as "a fragrant offering, a sacrifice acceptable and pleasing to God." The priestly service of the Philippians also consists of the sacrificial offering of their finances for the sake of Paul's work and the gospel's advance. They participate, in this unique way, in the ministry of the Word.

Thus Paul's writings help to fill out the picture of what royal priesthood involves in the New Testament. In Romans, the offering of oneself, conformity to God's ways and proclamation of the gospel are the central aspects of priestly ministry. In Philippians, any service rendered in faith and on behalf of the gospel is received as sacrificial service and a pleasing offering to God. What animates Christian priesthood is God's mercy in Christ; it is the fuel for carrying out our diverse ministries in service to God and his priestly people.

PRIESTHOOD AND NEW COVENANT WORSHIP: HEBREWS

Hebrews speaks a great deal about the priesthood of the church, and we will examine three key passages. First, in Hebrews 4:16 believers are encouraged, by virtue of Christ's high priestly work, to "draw near to the throne of grace" in confident prayer.[86] The verb "draw near" or "approach" is a cultic term, usually referring to priestly access to the sanctuary for the purpose of serving God's people, and the "throne of grace" refers to the Holy of Holies where God dwells.[87] Under the Mosaic covenant only the high priest was permitted once a year to approach the ark of the covenant in the Most Holy Place. Here in Hebrews, the "right of priestly approach," as one commentator notes, "is now extended to all Christians."[88] As a result of the preeminent priesthood of Christ, believers are now called into a priesthood in which they pray confidently, knowing they will "receive mercy and find grace to help in time of need."

The fact that it is the priesthood of Christ that opens up the way into the priesthood for his brothers and sisters is made explicit in our second passage, Hebrews 10:19-25. Believers enter the "holy places" and "house of God" through the "curtain" of Christ's flesh. As those baptized into a priesthood, believers are exhorted again to "draw near," "hold fast the confession of our hope" and "stir up one another to love and good works."[89] Taken together, these duties constitute the various aspects of believers' priestly vocation.[90] The first duty, drawing near, was addressed above (see Heb 4:16). The "hope" confessed (Heb 10:23) refers to the basis for Christians' hope: Christ's priestly sacrifice.[91] Believers perform their second duty as priests as they patiently and persistently rest in the work of the great High Priest. Finally, believer-priests are called to serve their Christian brothers and sisters by encouraging them to live according to their calling as those cleansed and consecrated. This provoking to "love and good works" occurs as Christians worship together and involves teaching and exhortation. The church is called to communicate God's words of warning, lest any fall away amid their trials through unbelief (cf. Heb 3:7–4:13). In the end, believers are brought into a priesthood by Christ's priestly work, initiated through baptism and called to carry out a variety of functions as part of their service to the house of God, the church.

Finally, believers live out their priestly calling as they love one another, show hospitality and visit those languishing in prison (Heb 13:1-3). They moreover show themselves priests by guarding holiness, seen here in terms of keeping the marriage bed undefiled, abstaining from the love of money and remaining steadfast against false teaching (Heb 13:4-9). The next verses make clear the basis for all such action—namely, the truth that the "altar" Christians have is far greater than that of the old covenant, just as Christ's blood surpasses that of animals (Heb 13:10-12). Since the sacrifice of Jesus is greater and lasting, the church is encouraged to offer through Christ, instead of blood sacrifices, the "sacrifice of praise" and the sacrifices of kindness and generosity to others (Heb 13:15-16). The phrase "the fruit of lips that acknowledge his name" (13:15) is drawn from Hosea and refers to worship, preaching and witness.[92] Priestly service thus extends to every domain of life.

To summarize, in Hebrews universal priesthood is rooted in Christ's priestly sacrifice, carries with it the privilege of access to God (particularly in prayer) and involves a call to service, composed chiefly of exhortation, teaching, fellowship and practicing holiness and obedience. As a priesthood set apart in and by Christ, the church is to live in the grace and mercy of God, rendering faithful service to God and one another with an eye to their eternal hope.[93]

A SUFFERING AND VICTORIOUS PRIESTHOOD: REVELATION

The book of Revelation contains three clear references to the royal priesthood of God's people, though much of the book's imagery is cultic or priestly (e.g., incense, prayers, altars). The first explicit reference is found in Revelation 1:6, amidst a doxology that praises Christ for his love for us, his liberating us from our sins by his blood and his making us to be "a kingdom, priests to his God and Father" (Rev 1:5-6). The last phrase is a reference to Exodus 19:6, but is here applied to the church as those who fulfill the call of royal priesthood. Christ's death and resurrection establish him as both "ruler of kings on earth" and priest (cf. Rev 1:13-18), offices in which he allows his people to participate.[94] Revelation 5:9-10 repeats the themes of 1:6. The Lamb is praised for redeeming people from every tribe and nation and making them to be "a kingdom and priests" to serve God and reign on the earth. This passage builds on both Exodus 19:6 and Daniel 7:22, 27 (Septuagint), the latter of which speaks of the church as those who are given a kingdom.[95] Here they are *made* a kingdom and given reign on the earth. Regarding priesthood, Revelation 5:10 simply asserts that the calling of the redeemed is to serve God. Finally, Revelation 20:4-6 speaks of the saints as reigning with Christ for a thousand years, a period in which they will also be "priests of God and of Christ." It appears from the use of the future-tense verb that a *future* reign and priestly ministry are in view.[96] Believers will serve their God in the new Jerusalem, which is a temple of sorts (Rev 21:21-27; 22:3).[97]

The manner of believers' royal priestly service, according to G. K. Beale, will reflect Christ, who as a priest reveals God's truth "through his sacrificial death and uncompromising 'faithful witness' to the world" and reigns as king by defeating death and sin through his shed blood and resurrection (Rev 1:5). The church functions as a royal priesthood when it faithfully witnesses to the world of Christ's kingship and priesthood. Much of the book of Revelation is an elaboration of how the church carries out its royal priestly ministry amidst persecution.[98] Being a royal priesthood involves heeding the words of John's prophecy (Rev 1:3; 22:7, 9), keeping Christ's word and not denying him (Rev 3:8, 10), holding to the truth of God's word even to the point of death (Rev 6:9; 20:4) and proclaiming the "testimony of Jesus" (Rev 19:10). Those who endure in faith and are not cowardly will reign with Christ as priests and kings (Rev 13:10; 14:12; 21:8).

CONCLUSION: THE BIBLICAL VISION
OF A ROYAL PRIESTHOOD

It is clear that Scripture has much to say about the priesthood of believers, more than might have appeared at first glance. As we have seen, the roots of this doctrine run deep, all the way to the very beginnings of God's people. We examined Exodus 19's foundational account of the kingdom of priests, stressing the privilege of priesthood as well as several requisite duties of priests generally, including sacrifice, reading, teaching, judging, distinguishing the holy and blessing. Our survey then took us to Isaiah and the promise of a restored priesthood through a priestly Servant. This promise is fulfilled through the ministry of Jesus Christ, one whom the Gospels depict as a priest and the founder of a priestly family. The rest of the New Testament—particularly 1 Peter 2, the Pauline letters, Hebrews and Revelation— fills out the details of the nature

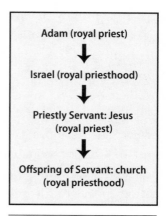

Figure 2.1. The pattern of royal priesthood

and calling of the royal priesthood, emphasizing the various priestly functions performed by believers, oftentimes within the context of affliction (see figure 2.1).

By way of summary, there are at least three themes that emerge repeatedly from Scripture regarding the royal priesthood of believers, and we present these as working theses.

First, *Christian priesthood is eschatological, reflected in Israel's corporate and professional priesthood but ultimately rooted in the church's familial relationship to Christ, the eschatological Priest-King.* Yves Congar writes:

> If there is one truth everywhere proclaimed in the gospel and Paul, it is that Christ is the firstborn among a great multitude of brethren, and that he communicates to many what he has accomplished for all. . . . He is priest and sacrifice, but

the faithful are priests and sacrifices with him—this is attested in more than fifteen passages of the New Testament.[99]

By virtue of our union with Christ, we share priestly access, privilege and duties with our Head.

Second, *the chief functions of the royal priesthood are to offer spiritual sacrifices, render temple service and proclaim the word of God.* As Christ, the living stone, offered the ultimate sacrifice, believers are called to offer the spiritual sacrifice of their lives, the totality of their being, to God. Our "temple service," furthermore, is the priestly service of building up the body of Christ through teaching, prayer, extending Christ's forgiveness and the deployment of our spiritual gifts. Proclamation speaks to the outward orientation of priestly ministry. Priests are to mediate between God and the world, and the primary way believers do this is through the announcement of the mighty acts of God in Jesus Christ.

Finally, *every member of the priesthood is called to active ministry in service of the gospel.* The promise of eschatological priesthood was to Jew and Gentile, male and female—everyone united to Jesus. As we saw in Philippians, the very gifts offered by common believers were received as their priestly service of the gospel. Priesthood is not the exclusive province of Paul and other professional gospel ministers; it is the shared calling of all believers, without exception. It is this full-orbed biblical-theology vision that helped shape the church's self-understanding for centuries and that fueled Martin Luther's retrieval of the priesthood of all believers at the time of the Reformation, as we will see in the next chapter.

3

PRIESTHOOD REFORMED

Luther's Burden

*But you are a chosen people, a royal priesthood, . . .
that you may declare the praises of him who called
you out of darkness into his wonderful light.*

1 PETER 2:9 NIV

Ø

I‍N AN EARLY WORK, *The Freedom of the Christian,* Luther
describes the glorious nature of our relationship with Christ as
a "royal marriage." He writes, "Who then can fully appreciate
what this royal marriage means? Who can understand the
riches of the glory of this grace? Here this rich and divine
bridegroom Christ marries this poor, wicked harlot, redeems
her from all her evil, and adorns her with all his goodness."[1]
Christ takes us to himself and imparts to us the greatest of gifts,
while we bring nothing to the table. Now this Christ, the bridegroom, is also the eternal king and high priest. Thus one aspect
of the "riches" Christ imparts to his bride, according to Luther,
is a share in these exalted offices. He states emphatically: "Now

just as Christ by his birthright obtained these two prerogatives, so he imparts them to and shares them with everyone who believes in him according to the law of the above-mentioned marriage, according to which the wife owns whatever belongs to the husband. Hence all of us who believe in Christ are priests and kings in Christ."[2] Believers are royal priests through our union with Christ! Marriage and adoption are parallels that help us begin to grasp this powerful truth.

There is little doubt that Martin Luther is the father of the Protestant doctrine of the priesthood of all believers. Admittedly there are many misunderstandings concerning his view, leading some, such as Luther scholar Timothy Wengert, to see the concept of the priesthood of all believers as "imaginary" and "mythical," a priesthood invented by the likes of Jakob Spener rather than Luther.[3] However, there is little dispute that the retrieval of the doctrine can be traced to Luther's reforms and, as we will see, it was a topic he frequently engaged in his polemics against the medieval church, even if he did not use the exact phrase. *Retrieval* is the appropriate word to describe Luther's contribution to the doctrine, for at least two reasons. First, it acknowledges a decline narrative of some sort. The doctrine indeed existed prior to the Reformer but suffered a degeneration in the medieval era. Second, it draws attention to the fact that this doctrine was not an invention of Luther's but something he sought to reassert.[4]

This chapter moves us from a biblical-theological discussion toward a more systematic treatment of the doctrine through the writings of Luther, who himself sought to weave together the various biblical strands highlighted in the previous chapter. In the process we hope to set the Reformer's doctrine in its context, dispel certain misconceptions, and bring out his positive, seminal and singular contributions to contemporary conversations on the priesthood of believers. To begin, we will spend some time tracing key patristic and medieval developments in the understanding of priesthood, as these set the backdrop for Luther's polemics and will help give us a feel for his concerns.

SETTING THE STAGE: THE MEDIEVAL PRIESTHOOD

We noted in chapter one that the New Testament does not speak of the church's ordained leaders as priests. We observed briefly the early developments that took place regarding priesthood in the writings of Tertullian. For example, in explaining who has the right to administer baptism he writes, "Of giving it, the chief priest (who is the bishop) has the right: in the next place, the presbyters and deacons, yet not without the bishop's authority."[5] Speaking derisively of heretical groups, Tertullian refers to presbyters and deacons performing priestly functions: "And so it comes to pass that today one man is their bishop, tomorrow another; today he is a deacon who tomorrow is a reader; today he is a presbyter who tomorrow is a layman. For even on laymen do they impose the functions of priesthood."[6] While, as mentioned earlier, the term *priest* was reserved for all believers, some early seeds were here sown for a new understanding of Christian priesthood. First, for instance, borrowing from Old Testament depictions the leading of worship and the offering of the church's sacrifices—particularly the Eucharist—became associated with the ordained ministry. Since worship and the Eucharist were then understood in sacrificial terms, it was easy to transfer priestly language to those presiding over these activities. Thus Tertullian nearly defines priesthood in terms of baptizing and the Eucharistic offering. Hippolytus (c. AD 170–236) furthermore speaks of the bishop as serving day and night, propitiating God and presenting the church's gifts and offering in the

Holy of Holies. For him, ordination sets one apart for a cultic ministry.[7] Second, there was a growing emphasis on the bishop's authority to forgive sins and exercise church discipline. Hippolytus, for example, stresses that the bishop's power to forgive sins is by virtue of his high priestly spirit. However, it was not until Cyprian (195–258), who became the influential bishop of Carthage, that these seeds grew to fruition and various underlying streams converged to produce an epochal shift in the church's understanding of Christian priesthood.[8]

Cyprian and the priesthood. There were at least two factors that allowed for this shift under Cyprian's influence. First, while church leadership structures indeed drew from Old Testament priesthood and its practices, imperial rule and other Roman political structures also became a key pattern on which they were based.[9] Second, and more important, church unity was paramount, since it was believed that unity was the only guarantee of continuity. By borrowing ideals and tactics from the Roman state, the church sought to defend its unity at all costs.[10] For Cyprian specific measures had to be taken to safeguard the church's unity. Eastwood writes, "In his teaching Cyprian entrusted this task to the bishop and to him alone. The bishop was the custodian of doctrine and the guardian of unity, and indeed the fulfilment of this twofold task was guaranteed because embodied in the person and office of the bishop."[11] The bishops, first, were the custodians of orthodox teaching because they were the successors of the apostles. Since Christian truth was handed down from the apostles to their successors, these bishops became the only ones who could guarantee the validity of the church's doctrine. Whereas in an earlier period matters of heresy and orthodoxy were submitted to the entire congregation for a ruling, with Cyprian the bishop became the source of orthodox teaching.

Thus the continuity of a pure church depended on the bishop.[12] Second, a bishop ensured the unity of the church in several other ways: he was granted control of the church's finances, he ruled the community and he presided at worship. He was also given special power to baptize, to confirm baptisms by the laying on of his hands and to bring people into communion with Christ in the Eucharist. Entrance and continuance in the church were dependent on the bishop, thus enabling him to wield unprecedented power in the life of the church.[13]

Regarding the bishop's relationship to the Eucharist, three innovations under Cyprian should be highlighted. First, Cyprian called the Lord's Supper the "sacrifice of the Lord." Second, he stated that the power to offer this sacrifice belongs to the bishop. Third, he held that the Lord's passion is the sacrifice that is offered. Thus under Cyprian the Eucharist became a sacrifice and the ministry began to be viewed as a mediating, sacrificial order, with the bishop functioning as the representative of Christ and priest of God.[14] Since the Eucharist occupied center stage in the church's worship, the bishop's power was consolidated through these innovations.

The issue of what to do with lapsed believers presented another opportunity to strengthen the bishop's power over the church. While rigorists argued that the lapsed should be excommunicated and the lenient party pushed for their reinstatement on the basis of certificates issued by Confessors, Cyprian sought to place the power of reinstatement exclusively in the bishop's hands. Only after a church's discipline was satisfied and due penance was rendered could a lapsed believer return to the church, and it was the bishop who imposed the satisfactions, determined their completion and pronounced absolution. Furthermore, as satisfaction of the church's discipline began to be identified with satisfying God, not only did entrusting reinstatement to bishops lay the foundation for the medieval indulgence system but it also gave the bishop alone the power to pronounce Christ's forgiveness.[15]

Cyprian therefore represents the beginning of the decline of the emphasis on all believers as a royal priesthood and the concurrent rise of the ministerial priesthood's prominence. Functions and appellations formerly ascribed to all Christians were applied to bishops and priests alone. Emphasis on the priestly race was being reduced to a priestly clergy who alone held priestly dignity and wielded the power of royalty. The *spiritual* sacrifices that once defined the universal priesthood of believers were replaced by the *actual* sacrifice of the Eucharist, which only the bishops and priests could offer. A new age of Christian priesthood had dawned.

Practical and theological innovations. As we continue this brief narrative, we would do well to take note of two related developments in the post-Cyprianic Western church's theology and practice of priesthood. First, ordination rites began to take on new meanings—moving from an emphasis on serving in a leadership office to receiving an "indelible mark" that created a separate caste within the one body of Christ. According to Andrew McGowan, the first detailed account of ordination is found in the *Apostolic Tradition*, a work likely compiled in the fourth century. Although we cannot claim any sort of uniformity in these practices across all churches, here we see evidence in the early centuries of the church of a practice in which the congregation would approve a candidate for ordination. Once approved the candidate would undergo the ordination ceremony, which involved two principal activities: prayer for the ordinand and the laying on of hands by leaders in the congregation (and sometimes from other congregations).[16] Of the two acts, prayer was foremost because the church held that God was the one who ultimately ordained. The heart of the ordination prayers was a request that the Holy Spirit empower the person to fulfill the ministry for which he was selected.[17]

However, the special gift of the Spirit on the ordinand eventually led to notions that he underwent a sacramental change. In the same way that sacramental prayers transform their respective objects, the prayer of ordination transforms a normal man into a graced individual. Augustine, in a treatise against the Donatists, asserts similarly:

> For the sacrament of baptism is what the person possesses who is baptized; and the sacrament of conferring baptism is what he possesses who is ordained. And as the baptized person, if he depart from the unity of the Church, does not thereby lose the sacrament of baptism, so also he who is ordained, if he depart from the unity of the Church, does not lose the sacrament of conferring baptism.[18]

Ordination, which is now explicitly referred to as a sacrament, confers on the ordained an irrevocable gift. Thus Augustine concludes:

> For as those who return to the Church, if they had been baptized before their secession, are not rebaptized, so those who return, having been ordained before their secession, are certainly not ordained again; but either they again exercise their former ministry, if the interests of the Church require it, or if they do not exercise it, *at any rate they retain the sacrament of their ordination*; and hence it is, that when hands are laid on them, to mark their reconciliation, *they are not ranked with the laity*.[19]

Whether or not the ordained man is in fellowship with the orthodox church or actually performs his office, he retains the
grace of the sacrament of ordination as an indelible mark (*character indelibilis*) on his soul. This mark separates him from the
rank and file of the laity, so that even after being officially disci-
plined for whatever reason he does not return to being a mere
layperson. This kind of teaching created a further cleavage between clergy and laypeople and perpetuated (and gave authoritative theological justification for) the decline of universal
priesthood and the concurrent rise of clerical power.

A second important development concerned innovations in
ritual anointing. Among early Christians anointing was associated with baptism and initiation, and they borrowed ideas
from Old Testament accounts of the priest's anointing and New
Testament accounts of Christ's. Baptism accompanied by
anointing initiated one into a royal priestly order. Over time,
however, in the West anointing became less and less tied to initiation and increasingly associated with ordination.[20] By the
eighth century the hands of presbyters and bishops were being
anointed at their ordination. This practice sanctified the hands
of the clergy in order to make them worthy of consecrating, celebrating and administering all of the sacraments of the church,
with special emphasis on the Eucharist.[21] Priests and bishops
were now *the* anointed among God's people. This change reflected already present currents of thought vis-à-vis priesthood,
but undoubtedly contributed to their calcification in church
belief and practice. Leithart concludes:

> The story of the introduction of anointing into initiation
> rites provides a cautionary tale of *lex orandi* leading *lex cre-
> denda* into a ditch. Though not inevitable, the development

possesses a powerful logic: Anointings were added very early to the primitive rite of water baptism; priestly meanings were attached to the oil; and, as the oil migrated from initiation to other ritual sites, priestly meanings migrated with it.[22]

This "migration" of priestly meanings from initiation to other sacraments was a sign that the priestly calling was shifting from every baptized person to a specialized group of people. As we will see, coupled with the sacramentalization of ordination, ritual anointing contributed to the cleavage between laity and clergy that characterized much medieval church polity in the West.

The post-Cyprian interpretation of priesthood may be summed up well by a letter from Pope Gelasius I (492–496) to the Eastern emperor on the relationship between sacral and royal power. He writes, "Two there are, august emperor, by which this world is chiefly ruled, the sacred authority of the priesthood and the royal power. Of these the responsibility of the priests is more weighty in so far as they will answer for the kings of men themselves at the divine judgment." He goes on to say,

Although you take precedence over all mankind in dignity, nevertheless you piously bow the neck to those who have charge of divine affairs and seek from them the means of your salvation, and hence you realize that, in the order of religion, in matters concerning the reception and right administration of the heavenly sacraments, you ought to submit yourself rather than rule.[23]

Two things are noteworthy about Gelasius's correspondence with the emperor. First, it gives potent and authoritative expression to Cyprian's understanding of the power of the clergy over all things spiritual. Second, it is a harbinger of an age when papal and clerical power would become incontestable not only by rulers but by all laypersons.

The Gregorian reforms and the solidification of the two estates. When Gregory VII became pope (1073), his early reform efforts focused on three areas: simony, the clergy's abstinence from bloodshed and clerical marriage.[24] The latter two emphases were important to Gregory because he believed the clergy not only had to be different but had to be seen as different. The issue with bloodshed concerned the clergy's direct involvement in battles, as well as their own exemption from physical punishment. Celibacy was also seen as a form of purity essential for men who handled the holy elements of the Eucharist; thus it became the most distinctive mark of priestly status.[25] After some success in bringing reform to these areas, Gregory turned to the issue of lay investiture—that is, the right of laypersons to install clergy. While Gelasius's interpretation of clergy-ruler relations was the official stance of the Western church throughout the Middle Ages, allowing the election of bishops and abbots by rulers was the *de facto* position.[26] This ongoing tension between canon law and actual practice exploded into what is known as the Investiture Controversy, wherein medieval popes and emperors fought over who had the right to install clergy. In 1075, Gregory issued a decree condemning investiture by laypeople, particularly kings, princes and other rulers:

> We decree that no one of the clergy shall receive the investiture with a bishopric or abbey or church from the hand of an emperor or king *or of any lay person*, male or female. . . . Following the statutes of the holy fathers . . . we decree and confirm: that, if any one henceforth shall receive a

bishopric or abbey from the hand of any lay person, he shall by no means be considered as among the number of the bishops or abbots; nor shall any hearing be granted him as bishop or abbot.[27]

Without detailing the events of Gregory and his successors' conflicts with Henry IV and subsequent rulers, what concerns us is the self-understanding of the Roman Church as expressed in Gregory's decree. The pope's statements, while limiting imperial power, in turn rendered all laypeople impotent. What was once a power shared by lay and clergy alike was placed firmly in the hands of clergy alone. Leithart insightfully relates Gregory's program to universal priesthood: "When Gregory defrocked the emperor and other political leaders, he removed most of the laity's remaining priestly vestments and confirmed the clerical monopolization of 'real' priesthood."[28] If Gregory's decree symbolizes the reality that the royal priesthood of all believers had all but faded in the consciousness of the medieval church, Pope Eugene IV's bull of 1439 provides an authoritative death knell: "Among these sacraments there are three, baptism, confirmation, and orders [ordination], which imprint an indelible sign on the soul, that is, a certain character distinctive from the others."[29] The clergy (and those in monastic orders) were the spiritual, the holy, the anointed and the powerful. To them were all spiritual powers granted.[30] It is in this environment that the voice of Luther resounded as he called the medieval church back to a proper understanding of the priesthood of all believers.

LUTHER AND THE SACRAMENT OF ORDINATION

Since medieval church life was inconceivable apart from clergy, a radical reassessment of the received understanding of priesthood lay at the very heart of Luther's reformation agenda. In fact, it was the elevated authority of the priesthood that largely fueled his emphasis on the priesthood of all believers.[31] As we have seen, the church tended to believe that clergy had absolute power over spiritual things. Consequently it was commonly held that within the church there were two "estates," the worldly (or secular) and the spiritual.[32] Luther inveighed against this notion and its very real consequences for church life. Since it was ordination that created the spiritual estate, Luther focused many of his attacks on the Roman sacrament of ordination and the sacerdotalism it seemed to underwrite. For him the sacrament was fraught with problems, the chief of which are the following: (1) it is not found or promised in Scripture, (2) it elevates the ordained to inordinate levels of power, (3) it creates a separation between clergy and laity and (4) it ultimately obscures, even denies, the priesthood of every believer.[33]

Unbiblical teaching. In an early writing Luther protests the supposed tyranny of the papacy, exercised through the misuse of the sacraments—especially that of ordination. He writes, "Of this sacrament the church of Christ knows nothing; it is an invention of the church of the pope. Not only is there nowhere any promise of grace attached to it, but there is not a single word said about it in the whole New Testament."[34] Luther does not recommend that ordination should altogether be abolished, but rather that the rite be presented as a *human* custom, not as something divinely instituted. For the church to promise some kind of special grace through their sacrament is to put the church in the place of God, who alone may make such promises. Thus Luther can assert: "It is the promises of God that make the church, and not the church that makes the promise of God."[35] For Luther, the sacrament of ordination is unbiblical both in its absence from Scripture and in the nature of the teaching it promotes.

Inordinate power. Luther was not opposed to the idea of sacramental grace as such. Rather, he took issue with the particular kind of grace purportedly bestowed in ordination.[36] As we saw above, Rome argued that ordination conferred an indelible mark on those ordained. Luther, however, rejected this tradition, calling the doctrine a "fiction" and a "laughing-stock." He writes, "I cannot understand at all why one who has been made a priest cannot again become a layman; for the sole difference between him and a layman is his ministry."[37] It is by this doctrine that two Christian estates are formed and perpetuated, since it permanently allows clergy to have spiritual power over the laity, including civil authorities. In the title of another of his early tracts, *To the Christian Nobility of the German Nation Concerning the Reform of the Christian Estate*, Luther therefore reduces the Christian estate from two to one.[38] In order to maintain their position his opponents shielded themselves from criticism, setting up what Luther calls three "walls." First, when pressed to change by secular authorities, they claimed that temporal powers have no authority over spiritual powers. Second, when others attempted to correct them from Scripture, they insisted that only the pope can properly interpret Scripture. Finally, if threatened by a council, they maintained that only the pope can convene a council. In this way Rome took away what Luther calls the three "rods" of the Christian—the church's very means of correcting and reforming itself.[39]

Clergy versus laity. To Luther it seemed inevitable that this dogma would nurture dramatic separation between clergy and laity. Conveying the heart of his concern, he writes:

They have sought by this means [ordination] to set up a
seed bed of implacable discord, by which clergy and laymen
should be separated from each other farther than heaven
from earth, *to the incredible injury of the grace of baptism
and to the confusion of our fellowship in the gospel.* Here,
indeed, are the roots of the detestable tyranny of the clergy
over the laity. Trusting in the external anointing by which
their hands are consecrated, in the tonsure and in vestments, they not only exalt themselves above the rest of the
lay Christians, who are only anointed with the Holy Spirit,
*but regard them almost as dogs and unworthy to be in-
cluded with themselves in the church.*[40]

Since the most significant things pertaining to the spiritual life
were in the hands of the ordained, laypersons often became
passive recipients of whatever was handed on to them. Therefore,
rather than promoting one common estate, this particular misunderstanding of the sacrament divided Christians into different
classes and did damage to the fellowship believers have in the
gospel.[41] Luther opposed Rome's priestly ordination largely because it divided the church. Further damage could result (and
did result) when laypersons began to believe that service to God
occurs only in the spiritual estate.[42] These problems arose from
a real misunderstanding regarding priestly ordination.

Luther's views regarding ordination encountered a problem:
the church fathers. His opponents rightly contested that the Fathers had elaborate ordination rites; therefore advocates of the
two estates were in continuity with the ancient church, while
Luther was not. In response, Luther contended that the Fathers
anointed with oil and added other trappings for the chief
purpose of making clear who was to exercise the office of

preaching and baptizing on behalf of the community. They clearly had no intention of creating a special class of Christians. Nevertheless, Luther did maintain:

> This good intention of the fathers and their consecration developed to the point where baptism and Christ were weakened and obscured by them, and there no longer remained a consecration to a calling or to the ministerial office, but it became a private consecration, ordaining private clerics for the private mass, and now at last it has resulted in a real division and distinction between true Christians and the devil's clerics.[43]

However well intentioned, the Fathers' additions to the simple ordination ceremonies of the apostolic era would eventually lead to the muddling of the true intent of the rite. Luther argued that according to Scripture, what his opponents called a priestly "estate" was no more than an office.[44] Vows of celibacy, anointing, vestments and tonsure—all of these additions conspired to exacerbate the breach between lay and clergy and were impediments to a proper understanding of priesthood.[45]

Denial of universal priesthood. All Christians share a single spiritual estate. They are priests—a reality not to be undermined by the existence of ordained leaders.[46] Luther writes, "There is no true, basic difference between laymen and priests, princes and bishops, between religious and secular, except for the sake of office and work, but not for the sake of status. They are all of the spiritual estate, all are truly priests, bishops, and popes."[47] Priesthood is the calling of every Christian and it is only from among this priesthood that priests (that is, ministers) are called to fulfill an office. Instead Rome ignored the common priesthood in favor of a special one. Luther, never one to mince words, goes as far as saying that those who become ordained priests willingly forfeit their natural Christian priesthood:

> For in carrying on their hateful office they make no one a priest until he denies that he was a priest before. Thus in the very act of making him a priest they in fact remove him from his priesthood, so that before God their ordination is a mockery, but also a veritable and serious degradation. For to say, "I am ordained a priest," is only to confess, "I was not, and am not now a priest."[48]

Luther was convinced that the reason the New Testament avoids using the term *priest* to refer to apostles or any other officeholders is to avoid this confusion. Rather than calling attention to the priestly ministry of every believer, "the pope has usurped the term 'priest' for his anointed and tonsured hordes. By this means they have separated themselves from the ordinary Christians and have called themselves uniquely the 'clergy of God,' God's heritage and chosen people, who must help other Christians by their sacrifice and worship."[49] Ultimately what was at stake for Luther was the very idea of what it means to be a Christian. That is, to be a Christian *is* to be a priest, with all the attendant dignity and responsibilities. Therefore, in order to uphold the common Christian estate Luther sought to correct his opponents' errors by a fresh examination of the Bible's teaching on the priesthood of God's people.

THE BIBLICAL DOCTRINE OF THE PRIESTHOOD OF BELIEVERS

Luther was well aware of the rich theology of universal priesthood found in Scripture, including many of the texts discussed in the last chapter. In fact, he builds his argument for the priesthood of all believers by focusing on three particular strands of the biblical material. First, he establishes Christ's royal priesthood and contends that Christians' priesthood derives from their union with him. Second, he examines the explicit statements in the New Testament regarding universal priesthood. Third, he observes the functions of Old Testament (Levitical) priests and argues that believers perform those very same functions in the life of the church. When these points are taken together, it will become clear that all believers in Christ share the same calling as priests.

Christ's royal priesthood. At various points Luther highlights that Christ's priesthood is Melchizedekian and therefore preeminent over the Levitical priesthood.[50] In fact, according to the Reformer, the Bible is emphatic that "we have only one single priest, Christ, who has sacrificed himself for us and all of us with him."[51] Christ, moreover, performs in a superior manner the other functions assigned to priests—namely, teaching God's Word and interceding for his people.[52] Luther derives these insights from Psalm 110:4, a central passage for his understanding of royal priesthood. Christians derive their priesthood from Christ's as "children" of the High Priest.[53] Taking his cues from the psalm, Luther asserts: "No one can be called a priest unless he has been born to this heritage of and through Christ, just as a child has its name and rights by heredity from its father. It is clear, therefore, that those who will be priests must be born as children of this Priest, and that those who are born of Him are, and are called, priests—all of them."[54] As these spiritual offspring participate in a common baptism, faith and Lord (Eph 4:4-6), so they share a common priesthood where acceptable service—in the forms of intercession and spiritual sacrifice—is rendered only through Christ who himself mediates and intercedes for us (Rom 8:34; Heb 9:24).[55] Thus the central elements of our priesthood derive their legitimacy from our union with and new birth in Christ, the High Priest.

New Testament statements. Not surprisingly, Luther's doctrine of the priesthood of believers depends significantly on 1 Peter 2:4-9. Much of his exposition of this text is found in his correspondences with a Catholic theologian named Emser, who accuses Luther of interpreting the text too literally.[56] Specifically, he charges Luther with teaching that all Christians are consecrated priests, when in fact the text speaks only of a common internal, spiritual priesthood. Luther concurs that Peter speaks of a spiritual priesthood and in fact nowhere deals with a consecrated priesthood.[57] The problem for Emser seems to be that Luther allots to this spiritual priesthood the very functions of clerical, or professional, priests. Thus because Emser imposes on the New Testament the then-current understanding of the term *priest*, it appears that the Reformer is arguing that all Christians should equally be made ordained church leaders, which is certainly not the case. Nevertheless, the apostle Peter declares that it is the whole church that is to be built up into a holy priesthood (1 Pet 2:5).[58] He further speaks of the whole congregation when he calls them a royal priesthood and commands them to proclaim the mighty acts of God. "[Emser] may interpret 'priests' as he pleases," Luther writes, "but all Christians are nevertheless such priests through this passage. If all of us should preach, then the tonsure-bearers must keep silent, since they have a different, special priesthood above all Christians."[59] External trappings do not a priest make. "Rather," Luther argues, "priesthood and power have to be there first, brought from baptism and common to all Christians through the faith which builds them upon Christ the true high priest, as St. Peter says here."[60] Thus 1 Peter 2 provides strong support for a spiritual priesthood shared by all believers, one that is characterized by the proclamation of the Word.

Other important texts in the New Testament for Luther on this topic include Revelation 5:9-10 and 20:6.[61] Both passages declare the same truth: all Christians are, spiritually speaking, kings and priests to God. In *The Freedom of the Christian* Luther claims that believers' kingship and priesthood flow from their faith, by which they rule over all things as kings and enjoy priestly access to God and may pray for and teach divine things to others.[62] For Luther, then, these three explicit New Testament references are clear foundations for the doctrine of the priesthood of every believer.[63]

Priestly functions. As the third aspect of Luther's argument for the priesthood of all believers, he contends that the New Testament assigns the regular functions of Old Testament priests to Christian believers, thus connoting that the latter are indeed priests. He identifies three chief functions: offering sacrifice, prayer and teaching the law.[64] Since we will be expanding on these and other ministries in the next section, we will simply allow Luther to summarize the main point: "Through these testimonies of the Scriptures the outward priesthood in the New Testament is overthrown; for it makes prayer, access to God and teaching (all of which are fitting and proper to a priest) common to all men."[65] The priesthood of all believers is thus a doctrine derived from a reading of Scripture that is attentive to Christ's priesthood, explicit references to believers' priesthood and biblical statements regarding the priestly functions granted to all Christians.

SEVEN MINISTRIES OF THE PRIESTHOOD

What does Luther deem to be the chief functions of believers as priests? We briefly mentioned three above, but here we expand the list of ministries Luther assigns to all Christians. One way he approaches this question is to take what his opponents, and medieval

Christianity generally, believed to be the functions of an ordained priest and show that all Christians are permitted to perform those very functions. In a piece titled *Concerning the Ministry* he identifies seven such priestly functions: (1) to teach and preach the Word of God, (2) to baptize, (3) to administer the Lord's Supper, (4) to bind and loose sins, (5) to pray for others, (6) to sacrifice and (7) to judge doctrine and spirits.[66] These seven priestly duties are, for Luther, various forms of the ministry of the Word of God, for, "we teach with the Word, we consecrate with the Word, we bind and absolve sins by the Word, we baptize with the Word, we sacrifice with the Word, we judge all things by the Word."[67] The striking move Luther makes is to extend this priestly ministry of the Word to all believers—men and women alike. He argues that if all Christians are given access to the same Word of God, and if all as priests are given a ministry—namely, to proclaim the mighty acts of God (1 Pet 2:9)—then no priestly duty should be denied any believer since they all derive from the ministry of the Word. Let's take up each of these seven practices in turn.

SEVEN PRIESTLY PRACTICES

1. *Preaching and teaching the Word*

2. *Baptizing*

3. *Administering the Lord's Supper*

4. *Binding and loosing sins*

5. *Prayer*

6. *Sacrifice*

7. *Judging doctrine*

First and foremost, preaching and teaching the Word is a ministry of every believer. Luther writes, "Even though not everybody has the public office every Christian has the right and the duty to teach, instruct, admonish, comfort, and rebuke his neighbor with the Word of God at every opportunity and whenever necessary."[68] Two things should be observed here, and these should help clarify some misconceptions regarding Luther's teaching on the priesthood of believers. First, he distinguishes between the *office* and *function* of preaching. Second, he gives every believer a *nonofficial* ministry of the Word. He is clear throughout his writings, especially against radical reformers who denied the validity of the pastoral office, that the public (or official) ministry of the Word is for those called by a congregation to perform this ministry on behalf of the congregation. He contends: "Although we are all equally priests, we cannot all publicly minister and teach," and "It is true that all Christians are priests, but not all are pastors. For to be a pastor one must be not only a Christian and a priest but must have an office and a field of work committed to him. This call and command make pastors and preachers."[69] Put another way, Luther distinguishes between "public" and "private" spheres, terms that denote the difference between official and nonofficial ministries. The priesthood of all believers obliges every Christian to declare God's Word in the private sphere—that is, to mediate the Word of God to fellow believers in personal conversation.[70] When a mother acquaints her child with the gospel, a brother teaches another the Lord's Prayer or, in fact, any Christian encourages or instructs others in the Word, there believers are truly living out their priesthood.[71]

Second, Luther permits all Christians—particularly in emergency circumstances—to administer baptism.[72] According to church law only ordained priests were permitted to baptize. However, like Luther his opponents allowed even ordinary women to baptize in emergency situations. According to their logic, he argues, every Christian is then made a priest since even ordinary Christians are allowed to baptize. And since baptism is a chief form of the proclamation of the Word of God, every believer is now given the honor of verbally *and* visibly preaching the gospel in the church.[73]

Third, Luther permits all believers in such situations to administer not only baptism but also the Lord's Supper. He argues from Scripture that the words of institution—"This is my body. . . . Do this in remembrance of me" (e.g., Lk 22:19)—were originally spoken to all those present at the Last Supper *and* to those who would come to the table in the future. Therefore the ministry that was given at that time was given to all. Likewise, when Paul writes in 1 Corinthians 11:23, "For I received from the Lord what I also delivered to you," he address all the Corinthians, suggesting that each of them is responsible for the meal.[74] Finally, Luther concludes that if the two greatest ministries—preaching the Word and baptism—are given to all Christians, it is no giant leap that all should be able to administer the Lord's Supper.[75]

Fourth, Luther holds that the "power of the keys" (the absolution of sins) belongs to all Christians on the basis of Matthew 18:15-20, which is spoken not only to the apostles but to all believers.[76] Binding and loosing are nothing other than the proclamation and application of the gospel. "For what is it to loose," Luther asks, "if not to announce the forgiveness of sins before God? What is it to bind, except to withdraw the gospel and to declare the retention of sins?"[77] The word spoken by Christ to Peter is the power behind every absolution; "indeed every absolution depends upon it," Luther exclaims.[78] Thus the power to forgive and withhold forgiveness is the privilege of all, since it is another form of the common ministry of the Word.

Fifth, prayer is the common right of all believers. Concerning prayer, Luther asserts that all Christians have access to God and may intercede for others. He writes, "We may boldly come into the presence of God in the spirit of faith [Heb 10:19, 22] and cry 'Abba, Father!' pray for another, and do all things which we see done and foreshadowed in the outer and visible works of priests."[79] Therefore, the numerous calls in Scripture to pray for one another only testify to the common priesthood of God's people. Luther further argues that since the Lord's Prayer is given to all Christians, all may take part in the priestly duty of making intercession for others.[80]

The sixth priestly function of sacrifice is also an activity carried out by all believers. Luther observes that already in the Old Testament the ordinary member of the community is spoken of as offering sacrifices in the forms of a broken spirit (Ps 51:17), thanksgiving (Ps 50:14, 23; 116:16-17) and righteousness (Ps 4:5). It is no surprise when we come to the New Testament to find that Christians are called to present themselves as a sacrifice to God (Rom 12:1), offer spiritual sacrifices (1 Pet 2:5), sacrificially put to death the misdeeds of the body (Rom 8:13) and offer sacrifices of praise (Heb 13:15). The only sacrifice in the New Testament is a spiritual sacrifice—that is, our bodies (Rom 12:1; 1 Pet 2:5). Luther connects this sacrifice to the Word of God in two interesting ways. First, the sacrifice is perfected by the Word, which means that it must be offered according to Scripture and as a result of the gospel.[81] Second, he interprets the Old Testament priestly sacrifice as the offering of Christians through the ministry of the Word. That is, the "office of slaughter and sacrifice signifies nothing else than

the preaching of the gospel, by which the old man is slain and
offered to God, burned and consumed by the fire of love in the
Holy Spirit."[82] Finally, this understanding of spiritual sacrifice
is tied to Luther's doctrine of vocation. According to the Reformer, our everyday work—farming, baking, parenting,
building—is a sacrifice of service to God, if offered in faith.
One writer concludes regarding Luther's view:

> The Christian brings his sacrifice as he renders the obe-
> dience, offers the service, and proves the love which his
> work and calling require of him. The old man dies as he
> spends himself for his fellow men. . . . The work of the
> Christian in his calling becomes a function of his priesthood,
> his bodily sacrifice. His work in the calling is a work of faith,
> the worship of the kingdom of the world.[83]

In all these ways, sacrifice is a priestly work to be carried out by
all of God's people.

The final function, the judging of doctrine, is a ministry of
the whole church, as affirmed by biblical passages that
(1) deal with testing false teachers (Mt 7:15; 16:6; 24:4-5; Jn
10:5, 27; 1 Thess 5:21) and (2) insist that every believer has the
Spirit of truth (Jn 14:26; 1 Cor 2:15; 2 Cor 4:13; 1 Jn 2:27).[84] The
testing of doctrine is an extension of the preaching ministry
in that it seeks to edify the church, not necessarily through
the positive proclamation of the gospel but by the refutation
of destructive teaching.[85] Luther exclaims: "It is the duty of
the Christian to espouse the cause of the faith, to understand
and defend it, and to denounce every error."[86] If every
Christian as a priest can preach the Word, the same may
judge doctrine. All believers share in the privilege and responsibility of rightly handling the Word of God.

LUTHER'S UNIQUE CONTRIBUTIONS

After setting Luther in context and providing some of his key biblical and theological arguments, we are better situated to draw out his meaningful contributions to the doctrine of the priesthood of all believers. We will highlight three. First, Luther helpfully dispels the myth of two "estates," and in doing so dulls the medieval emphasis on hierarchy in the church. The church is not so much located within the office of the ordained but where the Word is proclaimed, and this by all believers. There are not two classes of Christians—one tasked to *do* ministry and one tasked to *receive* it—but rather one single class charged with preaching and teaching the Word in its many forms. This does not preclude the fact that there are different manifestations of that common priestly calling. For instance, in a church there will be those who exercise the *office* of pastor or teacher as one expression of the priestly ministry. That one person has the charge of pastor does not detract from the priestly vocation of the congregation; in fact, the pastor is to strengthen the congregation in its priestly ministries (Eph 4:11-12). Thus the priesthood of believers is a death knell to *unhealthy* forms of hierarchy, particularly those that undermine the dignity and active participation of all Christians in "unofficial" priestly ministry.

Second, we see that the priesthood of all believers is not an affirmation of an individual's right to read the Bible and form private judgments, but rather has an emphasis on ministry to others. One Luther commentator captures the Reformer's view well:

> Luther never understands the priesthood of all believers merely in the "Protestant" sense of the Christian's freedom to stand in a direct relationship to God without a human mediator. Rather he constantly emphasizes the Christian's

evangelical authority to come before God on behalf of the
brethren and also of the world. The universal priesthood
expresses not religious individualism but its exact opposite,
the reality of the congregation as a community.[87]

Luther does not intend to create an individualistic democracy
within the church. While the priesthood of believers affirms the
dignity and right of every Christian to access God, it carries with
it the chief notion of responsibility. Christians have access to God
and his Word in order that they might minister the latter in its
many forms to one another. Luther's linking of the priesthood of
believers with the Word of God brings out the New Testament's
emphasis on the community and, in particular, the "one another"
aspects of the Christian's vocation. As a priest, the believer lives
for her Christian brother and sister. Luther even expands the
scope of believers' priestly ministry to include those outside the
church. One scholar concludes that, for Luther, the priesthood
of all believers is an affirmation of the mission of the community
to the world.[88] Preaching, absolution, baptism and the Eucharist
performed by believers all function to vocalize and symbolize
God's words of promise and hope to those still outside the fold.

These observations lead to a final, and related, contribution.
Luther is concerned that when the priesthood of all believers is
eroded the proper use of the Word of God is diminished. Though
the manifold Word of God might obviously still be proclaimed
by the ordained priesthood, its full effects, particularly its power
to reform and transform the church, are weakened because laypersons are not empowered to handle the Word as priests to one
another. What Luther suggests is that when the priesthood of
believers is rightly understood and appreciated it results in
opening more avenues for the Word of God to function more

fully in the life of the church. Thus in a sense Luther does democratize access to and ministry of the Word, but not to the exclusion of ordained ministers or to encourage individualism in Scripture-reading practices. Rather, he delivers the Word of God to every believer so that each is made responsible for the encouragement, comfort, edification and discipline of others, and all this for the benefit of the whole church.[89] In this context we are perhaps better able to understand one of Luther's most enduring contributions: his emphasis on translating the Bible into vernacular languages. We lose sight of how radical this idea was in Luther's day now that translations are so readily accessible in over a thousand languages. But in sixteenth-century Europe, the idea of reading the Bible in one's own language was revolutionary, even if not unheard of (e.g., Wycliffe's English translation). Indeed, the translation of the Bible into vernacular languages is one of the most significant aspects of Christianity's global story.[90] In his preface to the German Bible, Luther advises his readers to begin reading the Old Testament by thinking of themselves as priests and of Christ as the High Priest.[91] Luther's appeal to the priesthood of all believers may thus be seen as an affirmation of the centrality of the Word of God in the church's life. When one emphasis falls, the other is soon to topple.

Luther, in many ways, dismantles both hierarchical and democratic visions of church life. In their place he offers a vision of Christians as priests, carrying with them certain privileges and responsibilities. As priestly servants they live for the betterment of the church and the salvation of the world, bearing the joyful burden of announcing the Word of God to all in need. As this takes place, God works powerfully to reform the church and to continually conform it to the likeness of the great High Priest.

4

LIFE IN COMMUNION

The Trinity and the Priesthood
of All Believers

Great are the works of the LORD;
they are pondered by all who delight in them.

PSALM 111:2 NIV

THE MOST IMPORTANT THING about us is the God we worship, and the God we worship will determine the kind of royal priesthood we become. In short, we ultimately become like what we worship, and this is especially true for members of the priesthood of all believers. Christians serve a triune God—Father, Son and Holy Spirit. Why does it matter that Nicene Christians serve the triune God revealed by Jesus Christ? As a royal priesthood, we have direct access to God and are privileged to represent God to others and others to God. But our God is not the Allah of the Qur'an or the Ahman of the Mormon faith. Our God is a Trinity, and as members of Christ's royal priesthood we serve the Father, through the Son, in the power of the Holy Spirit.

When the Gospels' authors wanted to answer the question "Who is Jesus?" they answered with a story about the Father who sent Jesus and the Holy Spirit who empowered him. In a similar way, to answer the question "What is the Christian doctrine of the priesthood of all believers?" we need to explore the relationship between the Trinitarian God and his royal priesthood. Previous chapters have laid biblical and historical groundwork; now in this chapter we explain why it matters and what it means for the royal priesthood to worship, work and witness with a Christocentric-Trinitarian vision.[1] We also describe how the royal priesthood can appropriately respond to each person of the Godhead: Father, Son and Holy Spirit. Finally, we conclude with a few examples illustrating why it is important to maintain a Christocentric-Trinitarian balance as we preach and practice the doctrine of the priesthood of all believers.

DOES THE TRINITY MAKE ANY DIFFERENCE?

Why does it matter for the royal priesthood to hold to a Nicene understanding of one God in three persons? Consider three examples. Several months ago, Dorothy contacted me with a theological question (personal examples in this chapter are Hank's). She explained that she was doing a Bible-study workbook on prayer, and the study instructed her to pray to Jesus and ask Jesus to intercede for her before God the Father. This was confusing because she had been taught that as a member of the royal priesthood she could go directly to God without any mediator. Dorothy's question reveals an important theological reality for Nicene Christians: our goal must be to understand our prayer, work and witness in light of the fact that God is Father, Son and Holy Spirit.

Dorothy is looking for an answer from within the orthodox Christian tradition, but there are many versions of the priesthood of all believers, including non-orthodox ones. The functions and nature of a priesthood of all believers will be determined by the God that priesthood serves. Dorothy's answer would look different if she were one of the billion Muslims on the planet. A number of writers have noted that Islam's early advances were especially related to its embrace of a strong version of the "priesthood of all believers."[2] The god of Islam (*Islam* means "submission") is a monad, a monolithic deity, and this affects every aspect of how the Islamic "priesthood of all believers" functions.

Or consider The Church of Jesus Christ of Latter-day Saints. This non-Nicene group takes its "priesthood of all believers" far more seriously than most Protestant churches. For example, millions of adult church members wear a "temple garment" or a "Garment of the Holy Priesthood" under their regular clothes throughout the week. While Mormons are often teased about their "holy underwear," the doctrine sustaining this practice is Mormonism's version of the priesthood of all believers. Their doctrine is based on a sophisticated typological reading of the Old Testament's Levitical and Melchizedekian priesthoods combined with new religious revelations from Joseph Smith and other prophets. For Mormons, God the Father is also named Ahman and is not a person in the orthodox Trinity. Because the Mormon's God is different, the Mormon's doctrine of the royal priesthood looks different. For example, Joseph Smith taught, "While the sisters do not hold the priesthood, they share in the fullness of its blessings in the celestial kingdom with their husbands."[3] Only teenage boys and men participate in the Mormon royal priesthood; Mormon girls and women are not eligible. The God we worship will determine the kind of royal priesthood we become. Traditional Islamic and Mormon doctrines both reject the idea of a triune God, and their "priesthood of all believers" looks different as a result. What then are the implications of the Trinity for the doctrine of the priesthood of all believers?

THE ROYAL PRIESTHOOD IS
CHRISTOCENTRIC-TRINITARIAN

In the previous chapter we met Luther, the Protestant prince of the royal priesthood. He fought long and hard for the truth that believers have the privilege of representing God to one another and one another to God. For Luther, Christ's Melchizedekian priesthood as described in Psalm 110 was "the source of all Christian doctrine."[4] Luther was right, of course. Believers are only members of the royal priesthood because we have been united with Christ, the great Priest-King. At the center of a biblical doctrine of the priesthood of all believers is the idea of representing Christ through participation in his royal priesthood by means of the Spirit. Fred Sanders's Trinitarian axiom is correct: "*The more Trinity-centered we become, the more Christ-centered we become, and vice versa.*"[5]

But Luther lived in tumultuous times, and several factors contributed to his emphasizing in his later years what might be called a "binitarian" version of the priesthood of all believers.[6] His doctrine focused upward (access to the Father) and inward (believers as priests to one another). It remembered the Father and remained focused on representing Christ; however, it neglected an emphasis on following the Spirit in his mission in the world (outward). Three events in 1524–1525 (the Peasants' Revolt, opposition from the "enthusiasts" [*Schwärmer*] and the birth of the Anabaptists) led Luther to eventually avoid emphasis on the royal priesthood's participation with the Holy Spirit's activity in the world. One result was a tendency in Protestantism to neglect the importance of the Holy Spirit's leading of the royal priesthood to witness in the world.[7]

Learning from Lesslie Newbigin's "priesthood in the world."
If Luther tended to neglect the Holy Spirit's call to witness, who might we look to for a more Trinitarian version of the priesthood of all believers? Perhaps the best choice is Bishop Lesslie Newbigin (d. 1998). Newbigin was a missionary in India for forty years, where he served as a street preacher, pastor, church planter, ecumenical leader and bishop of Madras (now Chennai) overseeing one thousand churches. At sixty-five he "retired" to England, where he served as an inner-city pastor, college professor, speaker and author of some fifteen books and more than one hundred and sixty shorter pieces.

During the second half of his life, Newbigin was heavily involved with discussions around the *missio Dei* (mission of God). In 1951 he spent a week with theologian Karl Barth trying to understand God's sending of the church into the world. In 1952 he drafted the final statement for the International Missionary Commission's Willingen conference. This conference was among the first to wrestle with the Trinitarian nature of mission, and was also one of the first to popularize the language of the *missio Dei*. In 1953 Newbigin gave a series of lectures that were published as *The Household of God*. In these lectures he laid out why he believed a Trinitarian understanding of the church was essential for understanding what God was doing in and through his bride. Following these significant events, Newbigin spent the remaining forty years of his life working out a Christocentric-Trinitarian view of God's mission.

Pastor and theologian Michael Goheen has identified three stages in Newbigin's ecclesiology (understanding of the church). Before Newbigin began his missionary work, he viewed the Holy Spirit primarily in terms of the benefits the Spirit brought to believers. There was no direct connection articulated between the Holy Spirit and the mission of God. In his second stage, Newbigin saw that the Holy Spirit equipped the church for mission, but he emphasized what humans did in mission rather than what God was doing. In his mature third stage, Newbigin saw that all mission belongs to God (*missio Dei*) and that the Holy Spirit is the primary witness in the world. In 1978 Newbigin wrote, "In sober truth the Spirit is himself the witness who goes before the church in its missionary journey. The church's witness is *secondary and derivative*. The church is witness insofar as it follows obediently where the Spirit leads."[8]

While Luther's priesthood of all believers focused primarily on access to the Father and the privilege of ministry to other believers, Newbigin's doctrine of the royal priesthood is focused almost entirely on ministry to the world through the Holy Spirit. One evening in 1957 Newbigin "spent the entire night on the plane from Bombay to Rome reading right through the New Testament and noting every reference to 'the world.'"[9] His eyes were opened, and from then on he began to point out regularly that within Christendom the "priestly ministry of the whole body on behalf of the world has been tragically lost."[10] After this point, Newbigin's ministry included a strong emphasis on the church's responsibility to equip believers for their priestly ministry in the world. As bishop of Madras he sponsored regular conferences for different professions: medical professionals, government workers, lawyers, educators. At these conferences the main theme centered on how these believers could exercise their royal priesthood in the world through their vocations.

In what may be his magnum opus, *The Gospel in a Pluralistic Society*, Newbigin described six marks of a gospel-centered congregation. The fourth mark addressed the priesthood of all believers. The gospel-centered congregation is "a community where men and women are prepared for and sustained in *the exercise of the priesthood in the world.*"[11] Newbigin's greatest legacy may be helping Protestant churches of the West wake up to the vast mission field that surrounds them. As we awake, we begin to recognize that the Holy Spirit is at work all around us. He is leading every baptized believer in the gospel-centered congregation to participate in witness in the world (Mk 1:12; Acts 1:8; 1 Pet 2:9).[12]

What is a Christocentric-Trinitarian royal priesthood? We are making progress in answering Dorothy's practical Trinitarian question. From Luther we learned that a member of the royal priesthood must both represent Christ and remember her privileged access to the heavenly Father. From Newbigin we have seen that it is also vitally important to rely on the Holy Spirit's lead to bear witness in the world. A Christocentric-Trinitarian version of the royal priesthood begins its vocation with the Priest-King, Jesus. In short, the royal priesthood understands itself to be sent by the Father to share in the mission of the Son through the power of the Holy Spirit. Figure 4.1 illustrates one possible way to understand this reality.

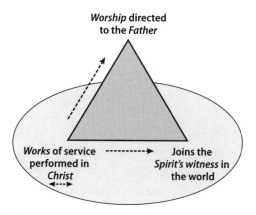

Figure 4.1. The royal priesthood and the Trinity

There are great riches in exploring the royal priesthood's deep threefold relationship to the Father, Son and Holy Spirit.[13] Figure 4.1 illustrates the royal priesthood's position "in Christ." We are only a royal priesthood because we have been united to Christ (the Anointed One) who is the Priest-King foreshadowed by Melchizedek (Gen 14:18-20) and promised to David (Ps 110:4). The majority of the book of Hebrews discusses the implications of Christ's royal priesthood. We are a royal priesthood as Christ's adopted siblings, and we share in his privileges and responsibilities (Heb 2:11, 17). As members of Christ's body, we have particular gifts that we use to build up other members of Christ's royal and priestly body. This is the "works of service" done by all members of Christ's body (Eph 4:12 NIV).

As members of Christ's royal priesthood, we can now approach the Father in the Holy of Holies. Through Christ we join our prayer and praises with those Jesus is already bringing to his Father (Rom 8:29, 34). To pray in Jesus' name is to pray in agreement with the prayer Jesus is bringing to his Father on behalf of a particular person or regarding a particular issue. The royal priesthood's relationship to the Father is especially associated with prayer, praise and worship, and the royal priesthood's relationship to the Spirit is especially associated with witness and the world. The Spirit is already at work in the world, where he provides the royal priesthood with opportunities for witness to the Son.

Of course figure 4.1 is not perfect. It does not reflect the realities of Christ's ascension or his promised second return (parousia). In reality members of the royal priesthood are only in Christ through the Holy Spirit, and the Holy Spirit is at work everywhere within and outside of the church. Yet this figure is useful in the way it helps us think about the ongoing relationship of

the triune God to the royal priesthood and the world. In the next
section we delve deeper into the rich relational dynamics among
the royal priesthood, the Father, the Son and the Holy Spirit.

THE BEST OF SONGS: THE ROYAL PRIESTHOOD RESPONDS TO THE FATHER, THE SON AND THE HOLY SPIRIT

The first phrase of the Bible's longest love song could be translated "the very best of songs." Solomon's love song celebrates a
beautiful relationship, and while its exact meaning has been debated for thousands of years, its picture of joyous love is a good
place to begin the story of the royal priesthood's relationship to
the Trinity. At its heart this story is a love story. It is covenant
love that calls and compels members of the royal priesthood to
desire a deeper understanding of our relationship with the
Father, his beloved Son and the Holy Spirit.

Leonard Hodgson (d. 1969) once described Christian maturity as being marked by a desire to grow in *"consciously* real-
izing our distinct relationship to each Person of the Blessed
Trinity."[14] John Owen (d. 1683), a Puritan pastor, shared a similar
belief. He was concerned that believers exercise "distinct communion with each person of the Trinity" and noted that for
members of the royal priesthood, "there is no . . . duty or obedience performed, but they are distinctly directed unto Father,
Son, and Spirit."[15] Owen wants us to think about our prayer, our
singing of hymns, our use of spiritual gifts, our witness in the
world, and to relate each action to the Trinity. Is this even possible? Where do we begin?

A few years ago I met Omar for lunch. Omar runs the research division for an investment bank. He is a smart man with
a sincere faith. As we headed to lunch, he asked me what I was
working on, and I described the question we are wrestling with

here: How do we as members of the royal priesthood relate distinctly to the Father, the Son and the Holy Spirit? While Omar had never explicitly discussed the topic before, he had a wealth of tacit Trinitarian knowledge. The way he prayed (in Jesus' name), read the Bible (listening for the Holy Spirit's voice), recited the Nicene Creed, sang songs, took Communion, was baptized and shared his faith all pointed to the deeply Trinitarian substructure of his beliefs about God.[16]

It is true that some in modern times have argued that an explicit knowledge of the Trinity is unimportant for maturing Christians.[17] But if a growing knowledge of the Father and an ever-increasing reliance on the Holy Spirit were part of Jesus' life, then they must also be important to the members of the royal priesthood. Recently theologians have again begun to emphasize the importance of thinking about the unique relationship each member of the Trinity has with creation.[18]

The royal priesthood's relationship with Father, Son and Holy Spirit. Loving someone well takes our best effort. Entering a covenant relationship such as marriage means we commit to working hard to understand our spouse. When I fell in love with my wife, Johanna, a couple of years after college, I had much zeal but little knowledge. I lacked a vocabulary and understanding of many practical aspects of her physical, emotional and spiritual makeup. After fourteen years of marriage, I have grown to understand the basics, but we both recognize I have a long way to grow if I want to really know and understand her.

Marriage between a man and a woman is a mystery—different of course from the mystery of the Trinity, but still a helpful analogy. Often believers begin a relationship with God with much passion and zeal. We don't know much, but we do know we have received grace, and this delightful knowledge fills us with joy. As we grow in our relationship with God, we grow in our knowledge of him—a knowledge with both cognitive and affective components. In this next section our goal is clear—we want to know God better so we can love and obey him more fully. Our love for God compels us to learn how we as members of the royal priesthood can best respond to the Father, the Son and the Holy Spirit as distinct persons. We are helped in this process with vocabulary and teachers found early among the sacred roots of our family tree.

Loving God in three persons: Some vocabulary. Remember Jesus' baptism? Can you see John the Baptist standing next to Jesus as he humbly submits to water baptism? You hear the Father's voice thundering across the water with words of blessing and a royal and priestly commission to his beloved Son (pointing to Ps 2 and Is 42). You see the Holy Spirit like a dove descending on Jesus with power for the mission the Father has just commissioned him to fulfill. How would you respond to each of these three persons of the Trinity? To answer this question it is helpful to make use of two time-tested theological terms.

Picture yourself standing with arms outstretched as wide as you can spread them. Of course your reach will never be great enough to grasp God—it's like trying to wrap your arms around a sequoia twenty-six feet in diameter. Karl Barth was a Swiss pastor and theologian who spent much of his life stretching his arms as far as he could reach toward understanding the Trinity. In one book he describes two terms essential for grasping the basics of triune life and love. For Barth, the right arm of his hug was the doctrine of appropriation while the left arm was the doctrine of *perichoresis.*[19] Both doctrines assume that ultimately God's work is a mysterious unity, and it cannot be divided. Appropriation is the older of the two doctrines, but both have been used by the church's pastors and teachers for more than fifteen hundred years to better understand the God we love and worship.

The doctrine of *perichoresis* (Latin *circumincessio*) has to do with the inner life of the Trinity. It has been described as a dance, in which the three persons of the Trinity mutually indwell one another and move with one another in love.[20] *Perichoresis* helps us think about God before creation. It provides resources for thinking through how the Father and the Son loved each other with the bond of the Holy Spirit in the eternity before there was created time, and it will continue to describe their relationship for eternity. While some theologians have looked to this doctrine as a resource for understanding how God's people should act, this approach has some problems, and the doctrine of appropriation can help us. It is better to begin with Jesus, as revealed in Scripture, when we want to understand how God's people should respond to the Trinity.[21]

A basic rule for understanding the Trinity is that the works of the triune God cannot be divided even though we can distinguish between the roles of the divine persons in these works.[22] Appropriation builds on the second part of this rule. Even though all three persons of the Trinity are always active in God's works, it is especially appropriate to associate the Father with creation, the Son with redemption (the cross) and the Holy Spirit with perfection and witness. Or again, it is especially appropriate to associate the Son with Good Friday, the Father with Resurrection Sunday and the Holy Spirit with the day of Pentecost. Appropriation helps us better understand and respond to God in light of his mighty acts revealed in Scripture. "Great are the works of the LORD, studied by all who delight in them" (Ps 111:2).

Appropriation helps the royal priesthood identify what a mature response to the Father, the Son and the Holy Spirit might look like. The doctrine can be defined as follows:

> Appropriation is a way of speaking about the God revealed
> in Scripture in which a divine action or attribute is assigned
> to a particular Person of the Trinity based on that Person's
> properties. The explicit goal of appropriation is to better
> manifest the divine Persons in the minds of believers.[23]

Returning to Jesus' baptism, we see that the mission of Jesus
begins with his Father who commissions him; the Father is the
source of the mission. The Son is the one who fulfills the mission,
thus revealing the *wisdom* of God. The Holy Spirit is the one
who provides the *power* for the mission. All three persons of the
Trinity are active, yet each plays a distinctive part.[24] Before discussing implications of appropriation for the royal priesthood
today, we first look at a few examples of how the doctrine has
been used in the past.

Loving God in three persons: Some family history. Thinking
about how the royal priesthood responds to the triune God is
not new; there are wise guides in God's family who provide a
reliable introduction. The African pastor and teacher Augustine
spent more than fifteen years writing his book on the Trinity. He
wanted to help believers understand God so they could love him
better. Explaining to his readers what lies before them as they
explore the Trinity, he writes, "Nowhere else is the error more
dangerous, the search more laborious, and *the results more re-
warding.*"[25] When Augustine and other pastors in the early
church used appropriation, they often emphasized specific *attributes*, which they appropriated to particular persons of the
Trinity. Other times they focused on specific biblical examples.
For example, Basil the Great (d. 379) discusses spiritual gifts in
1 Corinthians 12:11 and uses appropriation to help his hearers
understand the text. He explains that the Father is the source of

spiritual gifts, the Son is the sender of spiritual gifts and the Holy Spirit is the messenger who distributes the gifts.[26]

In the medieval era, pastors and teachers began to use appropriation to focus more on the *actions* of God within creation. They wanted to better understand how the Father, Son and Holy Spirit work within salvation history. Hugh of St. Victor (d. 1141) was the first to appropriate creation to the Father, redemption to the Son and sanctification to the Holy Spirit.[27] Later Thomas Aquinas would make extensive use of appropriation, and Protestant leaders such as Martin Luther, Martin Chemnitz and John Calvin followed his example. Using appropriation to guide the royal priesthood's response to God has proven fruitful in the past.

Loving God in three persons: the royal priesthood's response. Athanasius (d. 373), an Egyptian pastor and teacher, once explained that "the Father does all things through the Word in the Holy Spirit."[28] The works of God in the world have a grain, a direction in which they flow.[29] Appropriation helps us see this grain, and as it does it accomplishes its goal of better manifesting the divine persons to the mind of believers. In the previous section we saw that particular attributes and activities are appropriated to different persons of the Trinity. In the next section we look at how the royal priesthood can respond to each member of the Trinity in light of attributes and activities attributed to them by Scripture and theological meditation.

Praying to Dad, serving with Jesus, witnessing with the Holy Spirit. There are a wide number of Trinitarian appropriations that could be explored—indeed this section may simply provide a place to spark your theological imagination. The family of God has a rich heritage of thinking and living in light of the Trinity. In this section we look at three specific responses of the royal priesthood. We see why it is especially appropriate to direct worship and prayer to the Father as Creator of heaven and earth, to respond to the Son with works of service (ministry) directed to other members of his body, and to respond to the Holy Spirit by joining his witness in the world.

Praying to our Dad in heaven. One of the core classes at The Urban Ministry Institute (TUMI) where I teach is called "God the Father." Among other topics, the course looks at God's wisdom, transcendence and omnipotence. One evening as we were discussing God's sovereignty, a student, Devin, shared how his new understanding of the Father's sovereignty had released him from questions and guilt he had carried for years regarding a drive-by shooting that had killed his son. Even if Devin could not explain or understand the tragedy, he found new strength in meditating on God's sovereignty. The divine attribute of sovereignty, along with its closely related attribute of transcendence, has typically been appropriated to God the Father.[30] So also has the divine action of creation. Because the Father has the property of source, it is especially appropriate to recognize him as creation's source.[31] Thus, as the Nicene Creed states, "We believe in one God, the Father Almighty, maker of heaven and earth"; and as many pray daily, "you are the eternal Father, all creation worships you" (*Te Deum*).

How should the royal priesthood respond to our all-sovereign Father, the maker of heaven and earth? Is there a particular response especially appropriate to the Father in light of his attributes and action? Jesus, in both word and deed, has revealed insight into this question. He taught that it is especially appropriate to direct prayer and worship to the Father. When Jesus showed his disciples how to pray, he instructed them to pray like this: "*Our Dad* in heaven, hallowed be your name" (Mt 6:9; Lk 11:2, author's translation).[32] In the Gospels Jesus refers to his heavenly Father more than 160 times. There are eight places in the Gospels where we hear the actual words Jesus prays. Of these eight prayers, seven begin with Jesus saying, "Dad."[33] Paul follows Jesus' example and teaches that the Spirit now leads believers to cry, "Abba, Dad!" (Rom 8:15-17). When we meditate on the Father as the Creator, the omnipotent source of all things, we can pray with confidence that there is nothing too difficult for him (Mt 26:39; Lk 1:37).

Christians pray to the Father, through the Son, in the power of the Holy Spirit. What is true for prayer is also true for worship. When we were united with Christ through faith and commissioned to the royal priesthood at our baptism, Christ made us "priests *to* his God and Father" through his blood (Rev 1:6).[34] We find a similar theological grain in 1 Peter 2:5, where we read that the royal priesthood is called "to offer spiritual sacrifices acceptable to God through Jesus Christ." In the context of 1 Peter, "God" is especially associated with the Father in heaven.[35] Thus our offerings of worship are to be especially directed to the Father, through the Son, in the power of the Holy Spirit.

A word of caution is in order.[36] Jesus and the Holy Spirit are fully God, worthy of all worship. It is not wrong to pray to Jesus or the Holy Spirit. The work of the triune God cannot be divided, and there are places where Jesus clearly receives worship in Scripture (Rev 5:13). It is good and right to pray "Lord Jesus Christ, Son of God, have mercy on me a sinner!" Yet as we begin to think more deeply about the Trinitarian God, it becomes clear that it is especially appropriate to direct prayer and worship to our Father in heaven, in the name of Jesus, by the power of the Holy Spirit.

The Servant and his servants. At Taylor University where I attended college it was not unusual to play practical jokes. One night a prank war got out of hand. Human feces were spread across the walls on one of the residence hall floors. The news must have spread quickly, because before the maintenance crew had an opportunity to arrive the university's president and provost showed up with rags, rubber gloves and cleaning supplies. As college freshmen and sophomores walked out of their rooms that morning, they were startled to see the university's two most powerful leaders scrubbing their dorm's walls.

Perhaps the most astonishing thing about Jesus was his humble service. Isaiah's fourth Servant Song says that the nations will be "astonished" at the appearance of Israel's greatest King—the Priest-King greater than Melchizedek (Is 52:14; see also Ps 110). In Isaiah 56–66, the eschatological seed of the Suffering Servant are simply called "the servants." In an age when leaders would display their status with great pomp and ceremony, Jesus came as a leader who serves (Mk 10:45; Lk 22:27). He made it clear that his humble service to his disciples was meant to be an example for them to follow (Jn 13:15).

What is the appropriate response of the royal priesthood to the Son, the one who "emptied himself, by taking the form of a servant" (Phil 2:7)? One response is clear: we are to follow Jesus' example and offer loving service to his brothers and sisters. Each member of Jesus' family has received a gift that is to be used to serve other members of the family (1 Pet 4:10). Paul describes leaders in the church as those who equip Jesus' brothers and sisters for the specific "works of service" (NIV) or "work of ministry" (ESV) that each has been gifted and called to do within the body (Eph 4:12; cf. 1 Cor 12:7, 11; 14:26). Just as it is appropriate to focus our prayer and worship on the Father, so it is appropriate to direct our service (ministry) to others as unto Christ.

Paul often talks about believers as part of God's temple. Elsewhere he describes them as part of Christ's body. He constantly exhorts believers to consider how they treat one another in light of the fact that they are all part of God's family—his household. This idea of humble service to one another is rooted in Jesus' own life and teaching. To serve one of the "least of these," Jesus' brothers and sisters, is to serve Jesus himself (Mt 25:40; 10:40-42).[37] When believers build up the body of Christ they are doing "temple service." But strengthening the temple is not an end in itself; rather, the body is built up for its task of witness in the world.

The Spirit and witness in the world. As the royal priesthood turns *upward* in prayer, we especially direct our prayer and worship to the Father. As we turn *inward* to serve one another with love, our ministry to Christ's bride is appropriated as service to Christ himself. Finally, as we turn *outward* toward the world, we follow the Holy Spirit as he bears witness to Christ. After Jesus' ascension to the Father, the work of witness has been appropriated to the Spirit. "The Spirit is the one who bears witness" in the world today (1 Jn 5:6, author's translation; cf. Jn 7:39).

Bearing witness is not a new role for the Holy Spirit. From eternity past, the Spirit has borne witness to the love between Father and Son. Now the Spirit bears witness to the Son for the glory of the Father throughout all of creation. Jesus described the Spirit's ongoing witness like this: "When the Helper comes, whom I will send to you from the Father, the Spirit of truth, who proceeds from the Father, he will bear witness about me. And you also will bear witness" (Jn 15:26-27).

Just as the Holy Spirit led Jesus into the world to battle satanic powers and proclaim the healing presence of God's kingdom (Mk 1:12; Lk 4:1), so the Spirit leads believers into the world today. There is no corner of business, technology, medicine, education, politics, labor or any other vocation where the Spirit has not gone before the members of the royal priesthood (see

Ps 139:7). The appropriate response of the royal priesthood to the Holy Spirit is to rely on his power and presence as we bear priestly witness to God in the world.[38]

THREE INADEQUATE PROTESTANT VERSIONS OF THE PRIESTHOOD OF ALL BELIEVERS

Everything really good is in danger of being counterfeited, and the doctrine of the priesthood of all believers is no different. Counterfeit versions are inadequate because they are based on an inadequately Trinitarian view of God. Each emphasizes some aspect of the Trinity's relationship to the royal priesthood while neglecting other aspects. Three inadequate Protestant versions are described below. Each neglects the proper response to one of the Trinitarian persons, and together they illustrate why a Christocentric-Trinitarian version of the royal priesthood helps us respond appropriately to our triune God.

Clericalism: Monopolizing ministry to the heavenly Father. An old poem states, "The preacher in the pulpit, the layman in the pew, God made them very different, and keeps them that way too." The poem reflects an even older understanding of the royal priesthood. Medieval Roman Catholicism as practiced within Christendom largely suppressed the exercise of the priesthood of all believers. Martin Luther rebelled against this status quo by emphasizing all believers' access to the Father and their capacity for priestly ministry to one another. More than four hundred years later a Roman Catholic theologian, Yves Congar, completed a major theological study that agreed with much of Luther's emphasis on the priestly ministry of the people of God.[39]

Congar pointed out that for many centuries the church had failed to recognize the service of its lay members as what it actually was—namely, acts of priestly ministry. Congar sounds like

Luther as he writes that priestly ministries include activities such as "mothers at home catechizing the children of the neighborhood"; "the woman visiting the sick or prisoners"; "the organizer of a biblical circle"; "someone who initiates help to the unemployed, arrange[s] hospitality for migrant workers or someone responsible for the family hearth or for a course in basic literacy."[40] Congar's understanding of the priestly ministry of the whole body was endorsed by the larger Roman Catholic Church at Vatican II. While the Catholic Church continues to maintain a significant distinction between their ordained priests and the ministries of the whole priestly people of God, they have renounced a reductionist version of the priesthood of the faithful that monopolizes ministry in an exclusive clerical caste.

Unfortunately, within Protestantism there are still remnants of the medieval monopoly on ministry in some churches. For example, some continue to teach that *ministry* is a term that can only be applied to ordained clergy.[41] Like Levitical priests in the Old Testament, only a specific caste can be called "ministers" to the Father. Often proponents of this Protestant sacerdotalism are pursuing noble goals. They want to protect the dignity of ordained leaders within the church (see 1 Tim 5:17; Heb 13:7, 17). But as noble as this goal may be, denying a priestly ministry to all believers is the wrong way to pursue it. Those who deny the dignity of priestly ministry to the whole people of God fail to recognize the full implication of our eschatological age. We live in an already–not yet time—a time in which the end times have already begun. All believers are now ministers of Christ's new covenant. All have access through the Son to the Father in the Holy of Holies. All have been brought into God's family as holy ones and now serve as temple servants in God's house. As members of the royal priesthood serve one another in love, we also exercise a priestly ministry to one another. Luther and Congar were right to identify this privilege of ministering to one another as Christ's royal and priestly representatives as a foundational principle of the one, holy, catholic and apostolic church.

Atomistic and collective priesthoods: Misrepresenting our position "in Christ." While clericalism remains a concern, a far greater alarm needs to be sounded in this generation about individualistic perversions of the priesthood of all believers. I am reminded of a recent conversation with Derrick, a college student who told me he did not need to be a member of a local church. He claimed that his church was living with four other Christian college students. Derrick is not the only one who thinks the privilege of the priesthood of all believers means he can do his own ecclesial thing. Recently a popular Christian author has argued that millions of North American believers in Christ have wisely moved beyond participation in a local church. George Barna writes that "these people are devout followers of Jesus Christ who are serious about their faith," but they "grow in their relationship with God outside the ministry of a local church."[42] Barna lauds two believers who meet for "Church on the Green"; that is, their commitment to membership in a local body of Christ means that they meet to talk about life and God while playing golf on Sunday mornings.[43]

Derrick and George Barna have both made a basic theological error. They have confused what Roman Catholics and Orthodox believers call the "natural priesthood" and what Southern Baptists call "soul competency" with the doctrine of the priesthood of all believers. Natural priesthood or soul competency refers to an aspect of theological anthropology rooted in creation. All humans are created in the image of God; like Adam and Eve, they have a creation mandate to represent God to creation. This mediation of

God to creation is a priestly role. There is also an aspect of ultimate accountability in the concept. Each human will one day stand before God and give an account for his or her life. Humans are eschatological beings who will all stand before the triune God in unmediated glory on the last day. Each will be accountable for his own soul—there will be no proxies. Natural priesthood is rooted in these protological and eschatological realities.

In contrast, participation in Christ's royal priesthood is rooted in redemption, especially the cross. Only those who through faith and baptism have been united to Christ are made priests to God the Father (Rev 1:5-6). While conversion and the regeneration of the Holy Spirit is internal and personal, the closely associated event of water baptism is neither private nor individualistic. At baptism, a believer is commissioned to participation with the mission and ministry of the royal priesthood by a particular local body of Christ. This commissioning points to the human dimension of the priesthood of all believers. One cannot be an "atomistic priest," floating around and doing whatever is right in one's own eyes. As members of the priesthood of all believers we are called to exercise our priesthood within a local body of Christ. Christ loves his bride, and to be a member of his royal priesthood means to share this love as we fulfill our priestly responsibilities.

In the book of Malachi, God speaks a word of warning to the priests: "Oh that there were one among you who would shut the doors, that you might not kindle fire on my altar in vain! I have no pleasure in you, says the LORD of hosts, and I will not accept an offering from your hand" (Mal 1:10). While this passage speaks to Levitical priests, the warning remains relevant to members of today's royal priesthood. If we deny our need to serve as priestly members of a local body of Christ, then we are in grave danger of becoming blind to our own sin and, as a result, going about our priestly duties in a way that actually brings much dishonor to God. Theological writers warn about the danger of spiritual pride in this situation.[44] Spiritual pride is perhaps the worst form of pride. In it we assume that God's will is our will, and we make God our exclusive ally. We confuse our desires with God's desires, and we use God's name to justify our own desires and dreams.

In short, the reality of sin and spiritual pride should cause members of the royal priesthood to flee to the body of Christ. It is only as a member within a local body of Christ that we become free to exercise the privileges of our priesthood with confidence and maturity. In the next chapter we will look at seven marks of how this mature exercise of the priesthood can be identified. For now we simply warn again. It is impossible to exercise your royal priesthood in isolation from the body of Christ. Don't allow yourself to be deceived and to think that you can function as a member of Christ's royal priesthood by yourself. All of us need the body of Christ.

Before we move on, one other error must be mentioned. In some circles the danger of an individualistic priesthood of all believers is so feared that an individual aspect of the doctrine is completely denied. Proponents of this view argue that the priesthood of all believers is like Star Trek's imaginary Borg race—a collective with little personal identity or responsibility. In this view individual believers are not priests and do not do priestly things, but can only be considered priestly as a collective whole.[45] This collective understanding of the priesthood of all believers is just as inadequate as an overly individualistic and atomistic one. Our baptism commissions each of us to membership in the royal priesthood; however, the only valid exercise of this priesthood is from within the membership of a local church.

Holy egotism: Missing the Spirit's prevenient witness. The royal priesthood must continually return to the story of Jonah. It reminds us that our tendency is to forget that we are "bearers not exclusive beneficiaries" of the Spirit's blessings.[46] In medieval Christendom this tendency became especially pronounced. The distinction between the "church" and the "world" in everyday life broke down, because everyone in Christendom (i.e., Europe) was baptized. Emphasis on the Spirit leading the church on mission into the world was lost, and the church's focus became more and more inward. Elements of this medieval "holy egotism" were adopted uncritically into many branches of Protestantism, and it has only been in the last fifty years that conversations on the missionary nature of the whole church have been taken seriously by the wider Protestant family of churches.

Earlier in this chapter we looked at Lesslie Newbigin's important emphasis on the priesthood of all believers as a "priesthood in the world." His concern is that every member of the royal priesthood be proficient at proclaiming the gospel in his or her sphere of influence (see 1 Pet 2:9). The royal priesthood is gathered and built up by the Spirit of God for the sake of being sent into the world for the task of witness. Versions of the royal priesthood that rightly emphasize believers' access to the Father and priestly ministry to one another but fail to emphasize their priestly ministry in the world are inadequate.[47] The Spirit is already at work in every corner of the world, and he leads the members of the royal priesthood to participate in his witness to Jesus for the glory of the Father.

Newbigin explains that the appropriate response of the royal priesthood to the Spirit's prevenience or "previousness" is an obedient movement of witness into the world as we proclaim the kingdom of the Father and practice the healing presence of the

Son.[48] Members of the royal priesthood expect the Holy Spirit
to already be at work in the world; our task is simply to witness
to Christ in the power of the Holy Spirit in whatever place or
vocation we are led. Wherever we go, we believe the Holy Spirit
has already been there, bearing witness to Christ.

As we rely on the Holy Spirit's lead to bear witness to Christ
in the world, we are empowered to avoid the danger of propaganda. *Propaganda* is a technical term referring to a tendency
to preach the gospel plus our own contextualized church
culture. As I helped to plant a church among undocumented
immigrants in South Central Los Angeles, I became aware that
many of my ecclesial priorities were rooted more in my citizenship in the United States of America than in my citizenship
in the kingdom of God. For members of the royal priesthood,
our commitment to kingdom culture must always trump our
commitment to our culture of origin. As we learn to watch for
the Holy Spirit's witness in the world, we become better
equipped to join his witness to Christ. We also become more
skilled at distinguishing between our own cultural practices
and the essential truths of the gospel of Jesus Christ to which
the Holy Spirit empowers us for witness.

SUMMARY: MYSTERY AND MATURITY

The mystery of marriage can point us to a parallel truth about the
mystery of the Trinity. Recently my wife and I (Hank) had a long
conversation about some ways I need to grow as a husband. Even
if I have had to repeat a few grades and should be further along
than I actually am, the fact remains that I am more skilled in responding to my wife now than I was when we were first married.
Learning more about my wife has helped me mature in my responses to her words and actions. In a similar way, members of

the royal priesthood can grow in maturity and understanding as we respond to the Father, the Son and the Holy Spirit.

One often hears that after fifty years of marriage a husband and wife begin to look alike. Something similar happens in our relationship with God as we grow in our knowledge and friendship over time. Our God is a Trinity—Father, Son and Holy Spirit—and as our relationship matures, so can our responses. While we know that all of the triune persons are always working together, we especially appropriate creation to the Father, redemption to the Son and sanctification to the Holy Spirit. Attending to God's work in history leads us to respond to the divine persons with particular emphases. We direct our *worship* and prayer to the Father, through the Son, in the power of the Holy Spirit. We direct our *work* of ministry (Eph 4:12) as unto Christ himself, for the glory of the Father, through the power of the Holy Spirit. Finally, the Holy Spirit directs our *witness* to Christ, for the glory of the Father.

Recognizing the work of the triune God helps us mature in our responses and grow in our imitation (Eph 5:1). We will ultimately become like the God we worship. Growing in understanding of our triune God also helps ensure that our practice and preaching of the priesthood of all believers is worthy of the God revealed by Jesus Christ. In the next chapter we build on the Trinitarian responses just discussed in order to better understand faithful and fruitful practice. Throughout the family history of the church, a healthy exercise of the priesthood of all believers has corresponded with seven essential practices. These practices call for attentive reflection—to them we now turn.

5

The Practices of the Royal Priesthood

*So Christ himself gave the apostles, the prophets, the evange-
lists, the pastors and teachers, to equip his people for works
of service, so that the body of Christ may be built up until we
all reach unity in the faith and in the knowledge of the Son
of God and become mature, attaining to the whole measure
of the fullness of Christ.*

EPHESIANS 4:11-13 NIV

THE MOST IMPORTANT QUESTION in the last chapter was
"Who?" *Who* is the God the priesthood of all believers serves? In
this chapter the main question is "How?" *How* do we as members
of the royal priesthood faithfully and fruitfully respond to the
Father, the Son and the Holy Spirit? Throughout church history
(see examples from Luther in chapter three), seven "priestly
practices" have especially been associated with the royal priesthood's response to God. These seven central practices are
(1) baptism, (2) prayer, (3) *lectio divina* (divine reading), (4) ministry,

(5) church discipline, (6) proclamation and (7) the Lord's Supper. They may not be new, but examining them through the lens of the priesthood of all believers helps us exercise them faithfully in the varied contexts of our multicultural world.

"Begin with the end in mind!" This popular proverb points us to the New Testament's book of Revelation. There, as we have seen, the people of God are referred to as royal priests multiple times:

> To him who loves us and has freed us from our sins by his blood and *made us a kingdom, priests to his God and Father*, to him be glory and dominion forever and ever. Amen. (Rev 1:5-6)
>
> You have *made them a kingdom and priests to our God*, and they shall reign on the earth. (Rev 5:10)
>
> *They will be priests of God and of Christ*, and they will reign with him for a thousand years. (Rev 20:6)[1]

Revelation's eschatological vision pictures believers responding to the triune God as members of Christ's royal priesthood. N. T. Wright correctly claims that the ultimate *telos* of God's people is to "be the renewed world's rulers and priests."[2] Yet this ultimate kingdom vision can be embraced in the here and now. The seven central practices presented in this chapter lead Christ's royal priesthood more deeply into this apostolic vision of the early church. Before we discuss the seven central practices themselves, however, there are several preliminary issues to address.

HOW DO MEMBERS OF THE ROYAL PRIESTHOOD RESPOND TO GOD?

Miroslav Volf writes, "*at the heart of every good theology lies not simply a plausible intellectual vision but more importantly a* compelling account of a way of life, and that theology is therefore best done from within the pursuit of this way of life."[3] The doctrine of the priesthood of all believers provides just such a vision for the church today. Understanding ourselves as members of Christ's royal priesthood leads us into particular practices, into a particular "way of life." Those practices then shape the way we spend our time and how we view ourselves, the church and the world.

An ancient principle from the early church states that our worship (*lex orandi*) shapes what we believe (*lex credendi*). Our practice shapes our belief, and our beliefs shape our practice.[4] When believers have a clear understanding (vision) of themselves as members of the royal priesthood (1 Pet 2:9; Is 61:6), it can change how they view their practices. As their practices begin to change to better align with this new vision, the vision itself becomes understood and embraced at a deeper level. Another way of viewing this idea is to say our identity matters a great deal to how we live our life. When God rescued a slave people out of Egypt and brought them to Mt. Sinai, the first thing he told them was that they were to be "a kingdom of priests" (Ex 19:6). Their calling to be a royal priesthood was at the core of their new identity. As a royal priesthood, they were to live differently and embrace a unique set of practices in their world.

VIM and the royal priesthood. We now return to our opening question, *How* does the royal priesthood respond to our triune God? Dallas Willard, a pastor and philosopher, has laid out a general model for answering these kinds of questions. He calls it the VIM pattern, where *V* stands for vision, *I* stands for intention and *M* stands for means.[5] It provides a practical framework for understanding *how* we grow as members of the royal priesthood. Willard argues that all growth flows along the VIM pattern, but he is especially concerned with the spiritual growth of disciples in the kingdom of God. Consider a few examples of how VIM works.

Shamir, a seventeen-year-old, has just arrived in Los Angeles from El Salvador. She was sent to the United States to escape the Mara Salvatrucha (MS-13) gang, which is terrorizing the El Salvadorian city where she was born. Shamir has decided she needs to learn English as quickly as possible and immediately enrolls in English classes at a local community college. Notice that her actions reflect the vision-intention-means pattern. She has a clear *vision* of what she needs now that she is living in the United States—she wants to learn English. Second, Shamir has decided to learn English—her *intention* is clear. Finally, Shamir enrolls in English classes. She has identified a *means* to bring her vision into reality.

In contrast with Shamir, ponder a recent conversation I (Hank) had with Jose. Jose is a recognized leader in his church. He has over twenty-five years in full-time Christian ministry. But Jose has struggled with an addiction to pornography that goes back to abuse experienced as a small boy. Jose has a clear *vision* of what holiness and freedom from pornography look like. He has decided (*intention*) numerous times over the last thirty years that he would never look at pornography again. But Jose has failed to find a *means*, a plan, whereby he can live into the vision—the freedom in which he knows God has called him to live.

Ultimately, it will only be by the grace of God that Shamir and Jose will live into the visions they are pursuing. The Holy Spirit is the one who initiates and brings to birth all good gifts in our lives (Jas 1:17). But although the Holy Spirit initiates the vision, intention and means that bring lasting change, this does not mean that believers are passive in the process. "Grace is opposed

to earning, not effort," Willard would often remark. Our
tices as members of the royal priesthood are perhaps ᵥest
thought of as "activities of participation" rather than "activities
of achievement."[6]

How does this general pattern of spiritual growth (VIM) help
us respond rightly to God as members of the priesthood of all
believers? The answer is threefold.

*Vision: Representing Christ as a member of the royal
priesthood.* Walking out of the doctor's office after eye surgery,
I was amazed at how clearly I could see the world around me.
A right performance of the doctrine of the priesthood of all
believers begins with adjusting our sight and then fixing our
eyes on Jesus as the great Priest-King. After the cross, the
New Testament recognizes only one continuing priesthood.
It is the priesthood described in Psalm 110, the Melchizedekian royal priesthood of Jesus the Christ. As we saw in
chapter two, at his baptism Jesus was publicly commissioned
and christened to serve as Israel's long awaited Priest-King.[7]
After his baptism Jesus began to claim his kingdom with word
and deeds. The last days that Isaiah prophesied had come,
and now a servant-king was calling forth a servant-seed.[8] A
royal and priestly king (Is 53) was calling his royal and priestly
people (Is 61:6). The book of Hebrews makes it clear that
Jesus' royal priesthood is superior to all others (Heb
4:14–10:18), and believers are commanded to fix our eyes on
our great Priest-King (Heb 12:2; Ps 110:4).

Can you see him—the Son of David, sitting on the throne
surrounded by billions of royal priests shouting "Worthy is
the Lamb who was slain" (Rev 5:9-14)? Can you see him—the
Priest-King, clothed in his royal robe (Rev 1:13), walking
among his royal priestly family as they share in his meal, the

Lord's Supper? A vision for the right practice of the royal priesthood begins with seeing clearly the great Priest-King in whose royal priesthood we participate. At our baptism, we were publicly commissioned to share in the royal and priestly ministry of Jesus. Just as our baptism united us with his death, so it unites us with his present royal and priestly ministry. It is because we are united to Christ, by the Spirit, for the glory of the Father that we can now respond to God with the seven central practices of the royal priesthood. Our vision is to faithfully represent Christ, the great Priest-King, in our households and neighborhoods, churches and workplaces, cities and nations.

Intention: deciding to be faithful to our baptismal vows. At our baptism we publically covenanted to obey Christ, just as he publically confessed his obedience to his Father at his baptism (Mt 3:15). Responding rightly to God as members of the royal priesthood is simply to take seriously the vows we made on the day of our baptism.[9]

I (Hank) once heard a former missionary observe, "only those things done on a daily basis will ever dominate your life." Each day we must remind ourselves of our baptismal vows. Tertullian taught his congregation to think about their baptism every time they washed their hands. The covenant pronouncement we made before God and his people at our baptism needs to be called to mind daily (1 Cor 15:31; Heb 3:13). Members at the church I attend are challenged to daily remind themselves, "I have been baptized. I have been washed. I have been sprinkled. I am holy. I am commissioned. I have a ministry. I am Christ's royal priest." We are members of the royal priesthood because we are united to Christ. He is the Priest-King, and our royal and priestly practices all flow from our sharing in his ministry as the head of God's royal and priestly family. In the grace of the Holy Spirit, we must daily decide to walk in this truth.

A BAPTISMAL CONFESSION

I have been baptized.
I have been washed.
I have been sprinkled.
I am holy.
I am commissioned.
I have a ministry.
I am Christ's royal priest.

Means: The seven central practices. Just as Shamir and Jose needed practical means to learn English or overcome a pornography addiction, so believers need specific means to live into a faithful and fruitful vision of the priesthood of all believers. There are a wide variety of means that could be discussed, but the central means are clear.[10] The seven central practices of the royal priesthood are neither arbitrary nor optional. They are (1) baptism, (2) prayer, (3) *lectio divina* (divine reading), (4) church discipline, (5) ministry, (6) proclamation and (7) the Lord's Supper. These are essential for all who want to reach maturity in Christ's royal priesthood.

The seven central practices are both canonical and catholic. "Canonical" simply means they find their basis in Scripture. "Catholic" (or "universal") means that these practices have proven themselves essential for a faithful performance of the royal priesthood across twenty centuries and among thousands of cultures. These seven practices are evident wherever discipleship for all believers has been taken seriously (e.g., monasticism, pietism, base ecclesial communities). At its best Protestantism has been marked by these seven central practices since its earliest days. As we saw in chapter three, Martin Luther's essay *Concerning the Ministry* identifies a similar set of seven practices as essential for God's people (see table 5.1).[11]

Table 5.1.

Seven Central Practices	Luther's Seven Practices (1523)
Baptism	Baptism
Prayer	Prayer and intercession
Lectio divina	Judging of doctrine
Church discipline	Binding and loosing sins (bearing the keys)
Ministry	Offering spiritual sacrifices
Proclamation	Preaching the gospel
Lord's Supper	Lord's Supper

Notice that the seven central practices begin with baptism and culminate with the Lord's Supper. These two bookend practices are constitutive for the royal priesthood. One is the prologue and the other the epilogue.[12] They uniquely outline the believer's life as one united to Christ's resurrection life. They sum up the other five practices; indeed, they encapsulate all of life for members of the royal priesthood. Baptism is the public commissioning to the worship, work and witness of the royal priesthood, and the Lord's Supper is the ongoing means by which the royal priesthood publically renews its baptismal covenant vows. Proclamation and prayer also stand apart, as each of the royal priesthood's other practices could ultimately be viewed through these lenses. Before discussing further the seven practices of the royal priesthood, it is important to explain what we mean by *practice* and what we mean by *spiritual sacrifices.*

What Is a "Central Practice" of the Royal Priesthood?

The word *practice* can be used in different ways. On the one hand it could refer to a one-time soccer practice; on the other, to a doctor's or lawyer's practice. The way *practice* is used in this chapter is closer to the latter examples. A practice is something that is complex and communal. It is a response to God's grace with its own specific virtues and standards of excellence that embody a particular concept of the good (*telos*).[13]

For example, baptism is a practice that is, first, complex—it is made up of a variety of activities. There are activities related to the qualifications and preparation of the candidate and the community into which the baptized will soon join. There are activities relating to the ceremony itself—baptismal vows and pronouncements, submergings and sprinklings, sermons and symbols. Baptism is, second, a communal response to God's grace. It is a practice rooted in the grace of God. Everything about it, from the desire for baptism to the deep objective truths it symbolizes, is rooted in the mystery of triune grace. It is something done within a community as part of a "shared spirituality."[14] There is a long history behind baptism, and baptism integrates the baptized into a much larger community marked by the same practice. Third, baptism has particular virtues that are developed in those who embrace its pattern. Its practitioners work to develop the virtues of faith, hope and love. Fourth, baptism also has particular standards that mark off "good" baptisms from "bad" baptisms. A baptism done without faith or one performed under the threat of death (e.g., forced baptisms under Charlemagne) is an example of a bad baptism. Christian practices have their own standards of excellence, and while those standards are often debated, people who wish their baptism to be Christian must be willing to submit to the Nicene community's standards. Finally, baptism as a practice embodies a particular *telos*. *Telos* is a Greek word that refers to the "end" or "aim" of something. It is the purpose for which a thing is created. A hammer's *telos* is to drive nails, not to saw boards. The *telos* of all of the seven central practices is to form a royal priesthood to serve the Father, Son and Holy Spirit in worship, work and witness.

Much more could be said about practices, and the word may now feel overly complicated. But there are good reasons to make the effort to examine carefully these seven central practices. For one, our world today has become aware of the importance of culture and how culture affects our beliefs. Attending to practices can help us examine the interaction between the gospel, the church and culture in measurable ways. Thinking about practices can also help us avoid a "clerical paradigm" and instead focus on the wider activity of what the Holy Spirit is doing in the church and world. Finally, thinking carefully about the royal priesthood's practices can make concrete what many experience as an abstract doctrine.

THE SEVEN PRACTICES AND SPIRITUAL SACRIFICES

Disciples of Jesus Christ are those who offer their whole lives as living sacrifices (Rom 12:1). The royal priests serving in Christ's temple-house offer continual spiritual sacrifices (1 Pet 2:4-9).[15] These spiritual sacrifices are rightly understood as the offerings of royal priests who have been united with Christ through faith and baptism. All of life is a liturgy of praise for members of the royal priesthood; everything we think, say and do is ultimately to be offered as a sacrifice of praise and thanksgiving to God.[16] The connection between priesthood and sacrifices should be clear to most readers—priests are the primary ones who offer sacrifices. After our great Priest-King's sacrifice for sin on the cross, the only sacrifices his royal priesthood now offer are ones of thanksgiving and praise (Heb 13:15-16; 1 Pet 2:5).

If all of life is to be a response of thanksgiving, it makes sense that the central practices of the royal priesthood are also "spiritual sacrifices" offered to God. In the last chapter we identified how the royal priesthood responds to the Father, the Son and the Holy Spirit in specific ways. We continue to build on that insight in this chapter, but with the acknowledgment that ultimately all of the practices of the royal priesthood point to one God. Table 5.2 indicates that both prayer and *lectio divina* are especially associated with the royal priesthood's "upward" practices—those appropriately directed to the Father. The "inward" practices of ministry and church discipline take place within the body of Christ ("in Christ"), and are thus especially directed toward Christ. The "outward" activity of the royal priesthood, the practice of proclamation in word and deed, is especially appropriated to the Holy Spirit—the one who leads the church into the world to witness to Christ and bring glory to the Father.

Table 5.2.

Baptism	
Prayer	especially appropriate to the Father (worship)
Lectio divina	especially appropriate to the Father
Church discipline	especially appropriate in the Son
Ministry	especially appropriate in the Son (work)
Proclamation	especially appropriate by the Holy Spirit (witness)
Lord's Supper	

Just as the divine actions of Father, Son and Holy Spirit cannot ultimately be separated in the works of creation, redemption and perfection (*opera trinitatis ex extra sunt indivisa*), so the royal priesthood's response to God in each of the seven central practices cannot ultimately be limited to only Father, Son or Holy Spirit. The theological principle is this: the seven central practices of the royal priesthood cannot be divided between Father, Son and Holy Spirit, yet the royal priesthood's responses to God must preserve the distinction and order of the triune persons.[17] In sum, as we saw in chapter four, it is appropriate to associate particular practices with particular persons of the Trinity. Consequently, we think especially about the Father as we pray and about Christ as we practice church discipline, and we rely on the Holy Spirit as we witness. Learning to make these appropriations can lead to greater faithfulness and fruitfulness in the royal priesthood's present practice.

With preliminary matters now addressed, we turn to the seven central practices themselves.

SEVEN PRACTICES OF THE ROYAL PRIESTHOOD

This final (and longest) section of the chapter could be called "the royal priesthood's ethics in outline." It sketches out a brief introduction to each of the royal priesthood's seven practices. Baptism and the Lord's Supper begin and end the list as the commissioning and consummative practices of the royal priesthood.

Baptism: Publicly commissioned to the royal priesthood. The baptism of Jesus provides the foundation for Christian baptism, and this foundation is deeply rooted in the Old Testament's story of God's people. The New Testament's baptismal imagery draws on the waters of Noah's flood, the waters of the Red Sea as they miraculously parted with salvation for

Israel and crashed down in judgment on Pharaoh's army, and also on the water in which priests were "baptized" at their ordinations. Levitical priests were ordained for priestly service at the age of thirty, and it is not an accident that Jesus was "about thirty" when he was baptized (Num 4:3; Lk 3:23). The ordination service of priests, as mentioned in chapter two, is the only place in the Old Testament where a person is baptized by someone else (Ex 29:4).[18] The "baptism at Levitical ordinations lies in the background of John's baptismal practice."[19] Jesus' baptism was a commissioning service like Aaron's, and the commissioning aspect of baptism remains central to faithful practice today.

In many churches, baptism's commissioning to the mission and ministry of the royal priesthood has been misplaced or forgotten. The doctrine is called "the priesthood of the baptized" in the Eastern Orthodox church, and Roman Catholic writers such as Susan Wood understand clearly that the "priesthood of all believers is constituted by baptism."[20] But few contemporary Protestant pastors and teachers emphasize the present and future tenses of a believer's baptismal commission to the royal priesthood. Instead baptism is often exclusively discussed in the past tense. We must continue to emphasize the objective historical events to which baptism refers, but we must also recognize that baptism is "not over when it is done."[21] Baptism is a mystery as wide as the sea, as deep as God's grace. The next section will not try to say everything that needs to be said about baptism. Instead it focuses on one aspect—namely, baptism's importance as the commissioning service for the royal priesthood's worship, work and witness.

Jesus' baptism provides the foundation for Christian baptism. Why are believers baptized? The simplest answer is, out of obedience to Jesus' command in Matthew 28:19. But this command finds its basis in the story of Jesus' own baptism as recorded in the Gospels.[22] Martin Luther taught that to understand our own baptism, we "must enter the baptism of Christ."[23] Luther helps us understand that our water baptism connects us not only to Jesus' death but also to his life of obedience lived in the power of the Holy Spirit. Baptism is more than a backwards-looking event rooted in the ancient *past*; it publicly changes our identity in the *present* and commissions us to *future* mission and ministry as members of Christ's royal priesthood.

Just as Jesus' public identity changed at his baptism, so does ours. At Jesus' baptism he received a royal commission to fulfill both Levi's priesthood and David's kingship through a public anointing (*Christ*ening) to Melchizedek's royal priesthood. Jesus is a high priest after the order of Melchizedek—the first Priest-King of Jerusalem (Heb 6:20). In a similar manner, at our water baptism believers are commissioned to represent Christ as members of his royal priesthood. The dynamics of how this works can best be seen when Jesus' baptism is viewed in Christocentric-Trinitarian perspective.

Baptism in Christocentric-Trinitarian perspective: Matthew 3:13-17. Christian baptism must be understood in relation to the Son, the Father and the Holy Spirit. All three persons of the Trinity were working at Jesus' baptism. Take a moment to read Matthew's description of this great turning point in history (Mt 3:13-17). Try to imagine what it would have been like to be watching these events from the side of the Jordan that day.

> Then Jesus came from Galilee to the Jordan to be baptized by John. But John tried to deter him, saying, "I need to be baptized by you, and do you come to me?"

Jesus replied, *"Let it be so now; it is proper for us to do this to fulfill all righteousness."* Then John consented.

As soon as Jesus was baptized, he went up out of the water. At that moment heaven was opened, and he saw *the Spirit of God descending like a dove and alighting on him. And a voice from heaven said, "This is my Son, whom I love; with him I am well pleased."*

Then Jesus was led by the Spirit into the wilderness. (Mt 3:13–14:1 NIV)

What would have grabbed your attention first on that incredible day? Consider first the Father's booming voice: *"This is my Son, whom I love; with him I am well pleased."* What son would not love to hear those words from his father? But the Father's words were more than mere affirmation. He was pointing Jesus back to two passages from the Old Testament. Both are commissioning passages. As noted in chapter two, "this is my Son" comes from Psalm 2:7, a coronation Psalm—one used on the days when kings of Israel would begin their royal service. Its "twin" is Psalm 110, which describes one of David's sons who will be a Priest-King like Melchizedek.[24] The second passage is Isaiah 42:1. This chapter commissions the Suffering Servant to his ministry on behalf of Israel—a ministry that ultimately culminates in the sacrificial suffering described in Isaiah 53.

Jesus knew and had fully embraced Israel's ancient story. When he heard these words from his Father in heaven, the evidence indicates that Jesus understood their larger significance in light of Israel's story. His Father was sending him on mission. He was being commissioned to serve as Israel's long-awaited greater son of David—the true King of Jerusalem, the king after the order of Melchizedek. The baptism was the turning point of Jesus' life.

Consider, second, the baptism from the point of view of Jesus. While each of the Father's words at the baptism carries great significance, so also do the words spoken by Jesus. For Matthew's readers this is the first time Jesus' own voice is heard: *"Let it be so now; it is proper for us to do this to fulfill all righteousness."* The first words Jesus speaks are words that publicly announce his commitment to obey all that the Father has asked of him. Just as at a wedding a bride and groom say "I do" to fulfilling their covenant vows, so Jesus said "I do" to covenant faithfulness with his Father. The Father is calling Jesus to be the Anointed One, the long-awaited Christ, and Jesus responds with a clear commitment to live as a faithful covenant partner.

In a similar manner, at our baptisms believers make covenant vows to remain faithful to Christ. At baptism, after making certain renunciations most believers are asked something like this:

Do you turn to Jesus Christ and trust in him as your Lord and Savior?

Do you promise to obey and follow Christ as Lord: trusting his promises, obeying his word, honoring his church and showing his love, as long as you live?

In response to these questions, the candidates (or in some churches, their sponsors) respond with the baptismal vow, "I do!" Tertullian, an ancient African pastor, compared baptismal vows to the vows that Roman soldiers would take when they were sworn into the army.[25] Like the analogy to marriage vows, Tertullian's example helps us grasp that the promises we make on our baptismal day carry great significance for the future trajectory of our lives.

Finally, notice the activity of the Holy Spirit at Jesus' baptism. All members of the Trinity are active in Christian baptism. At his baptism Jesus is anointed with the Holy Spirit. In the Old

Testament both kings and priests were anointed with oil on the day of their coronation or ordination.[26] The anointing symbolized a new empowering from the Spirit of God for their work as leaders. But the prophets of the Old Testament also predicted a time when the Holy Spirit's empowering anointing would be democratized beyond these elite categories (Joel 2:28-29).[27] At his baptism Jesus is anointed with the Holy Spirit's power for the work the Father has commissioned him to do as Israel's Priest-King—but it is an anointing he will soon share with all who follow him.

Jesus' baptism brought the Spirit's empowerment for the ministry, mission and spiritual battles that would begin immediately afterward. In a similar way, a believer's baptism marks him or her as united with Christ. Recall Luther's analogy of the newly married bride and groom. All that belongs to the husband now also belongs to his bride. The union celebrated at baptism not only looks back to the death Christ died but also looks to the life he lives full of the Spirit's power. Just as Jesus was empowered for service as Israel's Priest-King, believers are empowered for service as members of the royal priesthood through our union with him. This priestly ministry is best understood as participation in the *missio Dei*, God's mission in the world.

Christian baptism is ordination by the Father to share in the royal and priestly ministry of the Son through the power of the Holy Spirit. This powerful truth must be reclaimed in our baptismal practice if the doctrine of the priesthood of all believers is to be performed faithfully today. Nicene Christian traditions understand differently the "how" and "when" of the Holy Spirit's empowerment in relation to water baptism. But all traditions agree that those who have repented, believed and been baptized have received the Holy Spirit and the gifts he brings to believers.

These gifts provide empowerment for mission and ministry.[28] They enable baptized believers to follow the same path Jesus walked—a path of worship, work and witness in a world often set in opposition to the will of the Father. Some traditions focus on spiritual gifts such as the fear of the Lord, knowledge, wisdom and understanding (Is 11:1-3). Others focus on spiritual gifts listed by Paul (Rom 12; 1 Cor 12; Eph 4).

Baptism is the entry point, the prologue to the ministry of the royal priesthood. Once we have been baptized, we are invited to enter into the practices of prayer, *lectio divina*, ministry, church discipline and proclamation. These five practices are summed up and renewed in our regular offerings of thanksgiving at the Lord's Supper.

Prayer: Speaking to our "Dad" in heaven. The first two practices of the royal priesthood, prayer and *lectio divina*, are practices orientated toward God. Both have to do with communication: prayer especially with speaking and *lectio divina* with listening. In one sense, everything we say, think or do when directed toward God could be considered prayer. Indeed one advantage of thinking about prayer as a practice is that it helps us to reflect on the many different activities and ways prayer can be approached (with fasting, in silence, in public, in private, etc.).[29] Yet there is also value in thinking about prayer especially as invocation—a calling upon the Lord in intercession or with thanksgiving. In the Old Testament the priests were given the responsibility to intercede for others and to offer sacrifices of thanksgiving. Their ministry of intercession was symbolized by the breastplate the high priest wore into the Holy Place on which were inscribed the names of the twelve tribes of Israel (Ex 28:29-30). It is also typologically prefigured in the paradigmatic lives of Moses and David, known as powerful intercessors. The New

Testament applies this royal and priestly responsibility to Christ. He is now at the Father's right hand interceding for us.[30] The basis for the royal priesthood's prayer is thus found in Christ, and we pray "through Christ, in Christ, and with Christ."[31]

As members of the royal priesthood, we were commissioned at our baptism to join with Christ's royal and priestly ministry of intercession. We are called to daily offer this service to God and to our brothers and sisters.[32] The priestly ministry of intercession before the Father is a great privilege and responsibility of the royal priesthood. It is exercised in specific and concrete ways—by singles for dear friends and coworkers, by spouses for one another, by parents for their children, by children for classmates and family members, by all believers for neighbors and coworkers. Royal priests intercede for believers around the world, for governments and for the will of God to be done on earth as it is done in heaven.

The royal priesthood's first prayer is the Lord's Prayer (Mt 6:9-13; Lk 11:1-4). Some ten years ago my practice of prayer was transformed when a friend, Terry, asked, "What if Jesus actually meant what he said when he told his disciples 'pray like this' and then taught them the Lord's Prayer?" The idea was new to me, but I soon learned that the Lord's Prayer is the touchstone for all Christian prayer.[33] Its use of first-person plural pronouns ("our") concretely addresses humanity's tendency to be self-centered. It balances familial intimacy ("Dad") with holy fear ("in heaven").[34] It teaches doxology and the seeking of God's kingdom as first priorities in our prayer. It encourages taking our needs to God, asking and granting forgiveness, and looking continually to God for deliverance from evil.

All prayers in the Bible "are summarized in the Lord's Prayer, and are contained in its immeasurable breadth."[35] Yet this does not mean members of the royal priesthood neglect the Psalms. The royal priesthood's practice of prayer begins with the Lord's Prayer, but it grows deeper with the daily rhythm of praying the Psalms. For three thousand years God's people have prayed from the Psalms, as Jesus' own example demonstrates. Just as a child learns to speak by repeating the words of his parents, so Christians learn to pray by repeating the prayers given by their heavenly Father in the Psalms.[36] The Psalms give royal priests the words to pray in times of rejoicing, sorrow, anger and thanksgiving. In previous generations it was not uncommon for believers to memorize the entire book of Psalms. One afternoon I spent time with a pastor who had done so, and his encouragement was to begin simply. "Start by memorizing a few of your favorite psalms and then pray those as you drive or go about your morning routine."[37]

Another idea is to choose one psalm each week and spend time daily meditating and praying through it. For a number of years I have used the Revised Common Lectionary's psalm of the week to guide my daily rhythm. The lectionary takes one through a three-year cycle of praying the book of Psalms. When we begin to pray Scripture regularly, we move into the royal priesthood's third practice—the practice of *lectio divina.* It is to this practice we turn next.

Lectio divina: *Listening to God as a royal priest.* Lectio divina is the practice of listening to God's voice speaking through Scripture. The ancient term, which literally means "divine reading," reminds us that when members of the royal priesthood approach Scripture they do so as part of a larger community whose tradition of hearing God's voice in Scripture goes back more than three thousand years. While the "reading" of Scripture has looked very different over the centuries, the faithful have always aimed at obeying the voice of Israel's covenant-keeping God. *Lectio divina* has had its ups and downs; by Martin Luther's day it was largely restricted to the monasteries. Luther was instrumental in breaking the practice free from this "Babylonian captivity." His leadership in translating the Bible into vernacular languages is one of the most significant aspects of Christianity's global story.[38] Vernacular translations were a necessary implication of Luther's under-standing of the priesthood of all believers. In his preface to the German Bible, Luther advised his readers to begin reading the Old Testament by thinking of themselves as priests and of Christ as the High Priest.[39] How should members of Christ's royal priesthood read Scripture in order to hear God's voice?

A priest was called to guard and steward the covenant rela-tionship between Yahweh and his people. This stewardship was especially important for Yahweh's words. As an oracular spokes-person, a priest was to inquire of God and speak God's word to the people (Lev 10:10-11). The idea of a carefully guarded cov-enant relationship is at the heart of the royal priesthood's practice of *lectio divina*. Members of the royal priesthood read Scripture differently than any other book because they are in covenant relationship with the book's Author. Consider an analogy. Today I opened a Valentine's letter from my wife. I read letters from her differently than all other letters because of the covenant relationship we share.

Covenant vows are an important component of baptismal practice, and those who have publically vowed to love and obey Christ read Christ's words differently than those who have not. The best description of covenant reading ever written is the acrostic poem found in Psalm 119. You can listen to it in about eighteen minutes. If you haven't read or listened to the psalm recently, take a break and do so now. Then reread a few highlights.

You have commanded your precepts
   to be kept diligently. (v. 4)
I have stored up your word in my heart,
   that I might not sin against you. (v. 11)
I will meditate on your precepts
   and fix my eyes on your ways.
I will delight in your statutes;
   I will not forget your word. (vv. 15-16)
Open my eyes, that I may behold
   wondrous things out of your law. (v. 18)
Your testimonies are my delight;
   they are my counselors. (v. 24)

In Psalm 119 and throughout Scripture, four virtues of the royal priesthood's "reading" of Scripture are described. These markers of covenant loyalty are (1) the fear of the Lord, (2) humility, (3) delight and (4) holy obedience. *Lectio divina* begins with these covenant marks.

**MARKS OF
COVENANT LOYALTY**

*Fear of the Lord
Humility
Delight
Holy obedience*

The first virtue, the fear of the Lord, is an acknowledgment that the one speaking in Scripture is the living God, maker of heaven and earth, of all things visible and invisible. Royal priests approach the Word with reverence expecting to hear the living voice of God (*viva vox Dei*). Augustine coached members of the royal priesthood that "it is necessary above all else to be moved by the fear of God" if one "earnestly seeks his will in the Holy Scriptures."[40] Psalm 119:120 puts it this way: "My flesh trembles in fear of you; I stand in awe of your laws" (NIV). For royal priests, *lectio divina* begins with the fear of the Lord (Deut 17:19; Prov 1:7).

The second virtue is humility. Members of the royal priesthood know that while we share in Christ's royal priesthood, we are not Christ. On this side of eternity we battle the flesh, the world and the devil. Our reading of Scripture reflects these influences that war on our souls. We recognize that every interpretive community has in some way been polluted by sin, warped by the world and deceived by the devil. This reality leads the royal priesthood to radical dependence on the Holy Spirit in prayer as we seek God's voice in Scripture. *Lectio divina* has classically required prayer as a constitutive part of the "reading" act. Psalm 119 provides numerous examples of this kind of interpretive humility. The Lord must open our eyes (v. 18), teach us (vv. 26, 33, 64, 66, etc.), give us understanding (vv. 27, 34, 73, etc.) and direct our responses (35, 133). For royal priests, humility is the "union card" required for all readers.

The third virtue is delight. "Oh how I love your law! It is my meditation all the day" (Ps 119:97). Royal priestly readers delight in God's Word more than a pile of gold or a million dollar shopping spree (Ps 119:72, 127, 162). It is delight in God's Word that leads royal priests to meditate on it day and night. Just as *lectio divina* has traditionally required prayer as one of its essential activities, it has also required meditation. A heart that delights in God's Word is the opposite of a heart that is "fat," callous or unfeeling (Ps 119:70). Delight ultimately results in the kind of exuberant praise expressed in Psalm 119. C. S. Lewis explains it this way: "All enjoyment spontaneously overflows into praise. . . . We delight to praise what we enjoy because the praise not merely expresses but completes the enjoyment; it is its appointed consummation."[41]

Fourth, the royal priesthood is a "holy priesthood" (1 Pet 2:5); its practice of *lectio divina* is marked by costly obedience. At his baptism Jesus said "I do" to the Father's commission. He became the faithful and obedient covenant partner where Adam had failed. To read Scripture as a member of Christ's royal priesthood is to recognize that when the voice of God speaks, his royal priests obey. Jesus modeled this holy obedience to the Father's voice, and it remains the cardinal mark of those who share his royal priesthood. Holy obedience grows from the fear of the Lord, humility and delight. As Abraham discovered, this obedience is often personally costly, and it is no easier at the end of one's life than it was at the beginning (see Gen 22).[42] *Lectio divina* is thus a dangerous way to read. Obedience to the voice of God in Scripture will often require suffering from faithful members of Christ's royal priesthood. This is true whether they are Coptic Christians living under an Islamic Caliph or North American evangelical Christians concerned about black lives, undocumented workers or unborn children.

The recovery of a faithful and fruitful practice of *lectio divina* in the church today is an urgent priority. Its traditional standards of excellence and the four virtues described above will guide a contemporary recovery of what faithful practice looks like in this generation. Dietrich Bonhoeffer suggested helpful practical guidelines for his students on how to do this in an essay titled "Instructions in Daily Meditation."[43] Others have suggested guidelines for the practice under the title "theological exegesis."[44] The exact activities will remain debated, but faithful performances of the royal priesthood's practice of *lectio divina* will result in fruitful work and witness, ministry and mission. On this note we turn to the royal priesthood's fourth and fifth practices—church discipline and ministry.

Church discipline: A key to the holiness of the royal priesthood. The previous two practices are directed toward God the Father; the next two are directed toward baptized believers *in Christ.* The practices of church discipline and ministry are directed toward "one another," and as such they are especially associated with the second person of the Trinity, Jesus the anointed Priest-King. In many North American churches, church discipline may be the most unfamiliar (and unpopular) of the practices. Naturalistic reductionism has led many to blame "sin" on social environments. Relativism has left many doubting any absolute standard for sin. Narcissism and a radical individualism reign in much of North America, and the idea of being accountable to others for our private actions sounds foreign to many.[45]

As we saw in chapter two, one of the central tasks of the Levitical priesthood was to guard the holiness of the covenant community—in some cases on pain of death. They were to guard holy space (tabernacle, temple), holy time (sabbath, holy days) and the covenant holiness of all of God's people.[46] In the New Testament the holiness remains central, but death penalties have been paid by Christ at the cross. Holiness is no less important now than it was when God first called his people to be a royal priesthood at Mt. Sinai (Ex 19:6), but death penalties now rest solely in God's hands (Acts 5:1-11; 1 Cor 11:30). The church is to be a place of both rigorous obedience and radical forgiveness.[47] Rather than the death penalty, an unrepentant covenant breaker is to be excluded from the church so that he or she can be the object of the church's missional witness. Although church discipline has been abused (e.g., medieval inquisitions, indulgences), this abuse does not negate proper use.

Historically the practice of church discipline (also known as "binding and loosing," "the rule of Christ" and the "ministry of the keys") has been a foundational practice for the royal priesthood. Martin Luther called it a "third sacrament" after baptism and the Lord's Supper.[48] Luther's retrieval of the truth that "the keys are yours and mine" released a powerful reform of the practice of church discipline and has remained a cornerstone of Protestant understandings of the priesthood of all believers.[49] Balthasar Hubmaier, an important early theologian in the Anabaptist communion, wrote that where church discipline is lacking, "there is certainly also no church, even if Water Baptism and the Supper of Christ are practiced."[50] Church discipline is a central practice for the royal priesthood, but how should it be practiced today?

An analogy might be helpful. One of my sons recently broke his arm at a soccer game doing a bicycle kick. The break was severe and the paramedics were called. It took three pediatric orthopedic specialists working together to set his broken arm. Setting the bone was intensely painful, but once the bone was correctly set the pain immediately lessened and proper healing began. When my son has the cast removed the doctors expect a full recovery. In contrast, one of my former students at The Urban Ministry Institute broke his arm as a youth and did not have medical insurance. His arm was never set and he has lived with a crooked arm for over thirty years.

Church discipline is as necessary for the body of Christ as setting a broken bone is for a young soccer player. Where it is lacking, limbs will never heal correctly and the body of Christ will fail to mature (Eph 4:15-16). As a practice, church discipline involves a complex range of activities including *instruction* on sin and the community's response to it, private or public *confrontation* of a particular sin, private or public *confession* from the sinner, *forgiveness* given by the person or persons who have been sinned against and the *restoration* of sinners as participating members of the covenant community.[51] In the midst of these activities, the Holy Spirit's virtues are developed in the royal priesthood—love, joy, peace, patience, kindness, goodness, faithfulness, gentleness and self-control. Love also doubles as an especially essential standard of excellence in this practice. The name for church discipline without love is frequently *abuse*.

The doctrine of the priesthood of all believers helps us understand that the vast majority of church discipline is not done by church leaders. Matthew 18:15-20, a central passage on church discipline, reveals that it is always to be exercised on the lowest level possible. In a church with a healthy understanding of the royal priesthood, ninety-nine percent of church discipline issues should never reach the elders, pastors or leaders of the congregation. When confronted by the brother or sister against whom I have sinned, I can confess my sin to that sibling as unto Christ (*in persona Christi*). Bonhoeffer explains:

> Our brothers [and sisters] stand in Christ's stead. . . . Christ became our brother in order to help us. Through him our brother has become Christ for us in the power and authority of the commission Christ has given to him [Jn 20:23]. . . . He hears the confession of our sins in Christ's stead and he forgives our sins in Christ's name. He keeps the secret of our confession as God keeps it. When I go to my brother to confess, I am going to God.[52]

Bonhoeffer is pointing us to the powerful core of the doctrine of the priesthood of all believers—we have been chosen by God to share in Christ's own royal priesthood. We have the incredible privilege and responsibility to represent Christ to one another and to the world. One of the most important activities in the practice of church discipline is "speaking the truth in love" to one another (Eph 4:15). This activity overlaps with the fifth practice of the royal priesthood, the practice of ministry within Christ's body.

Ministry: Serving other priests. In the Old Testament a central responsibility of the priests was to serve in God's house. At first this meant caring for the sanctuary and eventually it centered on service in the Jerusalem temple.[53] Jesus saw himself as the cornerstone of a new temple that God was building. This temple, made up of living stones, is closely related to the idea of royal priesthood. In 1 Peter 2:4-9 the themes of royal priesthood, temple and the offering of spiritual sacrifices are woven together to describe the identity of God's holy people. Those who are part of Christ's body live and work as members of his eschatological temple—and in the world of the first century, anyone who worked in a temple while offering "spiritual" sacrifices could easily be identified as a priest.

In Ephesians 4:12, the "work" that each believer is called to do in order to build up the body of Christ is called service (*diakonia*). Based off this verse, we are calling the practices directed toward those *in Christ*—church discipline and ministry—the *work* of the royal priesthood. Jesus surprised the whole world by revealing himself as a king who was humble and meek as a servant. He took on the lowliest of roles, washing his disciples' feet, as an example for his disciples to imitate (Jn 13). Believers engage in ministry when they participate through the Spirit's power in practical service to the saints. This service is performed as each member does his or her part, using the gifts they have been given for the building up of the rest of the body (1 Cor 12:7; 1 Pet 4:10-11). In addition to using their unique gifts and vocations to serve the body, every member is called to speak "the truth in love" (Eph 4:15), to "instruct one another" (Rom 15:14), to teach and admonish one another (Col 3:16) and to "exhort one another" (Heb 3:13). Every member of the royal priesthood is compelled by love for Christ to engage in ministry, but we also recognize that it is a responsibility he has given to all who through baptism have covenanted to obey his command to thankful service.[54]

In some Protestant circles the term *ministry* has been limited to a practice performed exclusively by the clergy or leadership of the church. This reductionist understanding of the practice of ministry has caused great harm to a faithful performance of the royal priesthood. The ministry of church leaders is an absolutely essential activity in the larger practice of the royal priesthood's ministry. Ephesians 4:11-12 explains that leaders in the church are the ones who equip the members of the royal priesthood to do the work of the ministry. Without leaders performing their ministry, the rest of the royal priesthood will never grow into the "fullness of Christ," displaying Christ's beauty to a broken world (Eph 4:13).[55]

Every-member ministry is a vital practice of the royal priesthood. It builds on the practices that have come before. Believers are commissioned to ministry at their baptism. As they engage in the practices of prayer and *lectio divina* in the context of the local church, they are directed by the voice of God to the specific work of service they have uniquely been called to within the body of Christ. As they engage in the practice of church discipline, members of the royal priesthood help to heal the brokenness experienced by all believers due to the flesh, the world and the devil. But the royal priesthood's practices do not terminate in ministry within the body of Christ. Rather, they have a centrifugal force leading to the practice of proclamation. The fruit of the royal priesthood's ministry is designed to be shared with a world that is starving. Recognizing the missionary nature of all the royal priesthood's practices is foundational to their faithful performance. All of them are bound up in the *missio Dei*—the Father's sending of the Son and the Spirit to bring salvation and shalom to the whole world. We will return to a brief discussion of the interconnectedness of the royal priesthood's work, witness and worship in the conclusion. But first we turn to proclamation, the royal priesthood's outward-directed practice.

Proclamation: The royal priesthood's witness in word and deed. Witness provides the third category for the royal priesthood's practices. Whereas worship is directed toward the Father and work toward the Son, *witness* describes the direction of the royal priesthood's response to the Holy Spirit's prevenience in the world. The practice of proclamation recognizes that the Holy Spirit has gone before the royal priesthood into the world to bear witness to Christ for the glory of the Father. The key text for the royal priesthood's practice is 1 Peter 2:9: "You are a chosen race, a royal priesthood . . . that you may proclaim the excellencies of him who called you out of darkness into his marvelous light." Paul says something similar, explaining that the mission of God's holy and priestly people is to shine as lights while holding forth the word of life (Phil 2:15-16).[56]

The proclamation of the royal priesthood is marked by the virtue of bold humility—even in the face of potential suffering. Lesslie Newbigin likens proclamation to a witness who is called to speak at a trial. Ultimately the truth will be revealed and a final verdict made. In the meantime the royal priesthood's responsibility is to proclaim the truth in word and deed to a watching world. This proclamation takes place as the royal priesthood serves as a "sign, foretaste, and instrument of the kingdom."[57] Life in the kingdom is life in the footsteps of Jesus—a path that has often led faithful practitioners of proclamation into costly suffering (Heb 12:2).

Proclamation is also especially concerned with the poor, with those who are sick or hungry, with those oppressed by social structures and with those oppressed by demonic powers (Is 58; 66:2; Mt 5:3). In the Old Testament priests were called to serve as guardians and stewards for the poor (Deut 14:28–15:18), and the temple was to be a place of justice for the oppressed.[58] It is to those who are poor that the gospel comes as especially good news. And care for the poor was to be a distinguishing mark of the holiness of the covenant community (Jas 1:27).

A faithful performance of the practice of proclamation cannot separate word and deed. Fifty years ago evangelicals tended to neglect deeds in carrying out their mission; today they tend to neglect words. Deeds need words to disambiguate them and to make sure that they point to Christ's kingdom rather than our own. Words need deeds lest they prove empty of power and a hollow mockery of the kingdom to which they testify. A division between word and deed in the royal priesthood's proclamation is a relatively recent product of history (from the last one hundred years), and this division has largely been associated with "white" versions of fundamentalism and evangelicalism. In the Latino church, the unity of word and deed is assumed and the practice of proclamation is often termed *integral mission*.[59] In African American churches, word and deed almost always go hand in hand. The civil rights movement in the 1960s offers a beautiful picture of this integration as the black church marched to protest injustice (deed) while singing hymns and songs of praise to Jesus (word).

The practice of proclamation is complex. There are many activities that can be involved: preaching, personal evangelism, incarnational evangelism, attractional evangelism, integral evangelism, evangelization, centripetal mission, social justice, spiritual warfare, creation care (see Mk 16:15) or simply loving your neighbor.[60] But ultimately all these activities find their aim in testifying to Christ and his kingdom in the power of the Holy Spirit for the glory of the Father.

The Lord's Supper: Culmination of the royal priesthood's practices. The Lord's Supper, or *Eucharist* as it has been known throughout much of church history, is the culmination of the royal priesthood's seven practices.[61] Thomas Aquinas taught that the Lord's Supper was the "greatest of all the sacraments . . . all the other sacraments are ordered to this one as to their end."[62] Many Protestant churches have lost this sense of appreciation for the Lord's Supper. Many times it is a rarely used appendix to a monthly or quarterly worship gathering. This was not the case in the early church. Everett Ferguson explains, "Both theologically and sociologically, the Lord's Supper was the central act of the *weekly* assemblies of the early church"[63] Note the word *weekly*. The testimony of the New Testament documents and the teachings of the patristic writers, the medieval doctors, the vast majority of Reformation and post-Reformation pastors (Luther, Calvin, Edwards, Wesley, etc.), as well as the continuous practice of many church communions, demonstrates the importance of a weekly celebration of the Lord's Supper.

Perhaps this generation will be the one that returns to a weekly celebration of the Lord's Supper as standard practice in Protestant churches. As the seventh practice of the royal priesthood, the Lord's Supper is the paradigmatic spiritual sacrifice of thanksgiving offered by the royal priesthood to the Father, through the

Son, by the Holy Spirit. It provides the model for offering all of the royal priesthood's practices back to the Father as a spiritual sacrifice of thanksgiving. The actual activities that make up the practice of the Lord's Supper are displayed in diverse and beautiful ways across countless cultures and languages (see Rev 5:9-10).

Gordon Smith provides a helpful overview of the Lord's Supper using seven words: remembrance, forgiveness, Eucharist, covenant, communion, nourishment and anticipation.[64] These words help us to think about the Supper's past, present and future components. They can also be thought of as standards of excellence, helping us to evaluate our own activities as we practice the Lord's Supper in our own local context. Remembrance, forgiveness, Eucharist and covenant all point to the past—even as they continue to shape the present. Communion (or fellowship) and nourishment remind us of what the Holy Spirit is doing in the present as we participate in the Lord's Supper. Anticipation directs our attention into the future as we consider the eschatological dimension of the meal.

THE MEANING OF THE LORD'S SUPPER IN SEVEN WORDS

Remembrance

Forgiveness

Eucharist

Covenant

Communion

Nourishment

Anticipation

From Gordon T. Smith, **A Holy Meal: The Lord's Supper in the Life of the Church** *(Grand Rapids: Baker Academic, 2005).*

The Lord's Supper, like baptism, is a deep mystery of grace. Each time we partake of it we are invited to taste and see the depth of the riches of the gospel. The good news of God's kingdom is displayed as the family of God comes together to share the family meal. We remember our great King who has made us a royal priesthood (1 Cor 11:24; Rev 1:6). We find the power to forgive as we have been forgiven (Mt 6:12; 26:28).[65] We celebrate our sharing in the royal and priestly ministry of the new covenant (2 Cor 3:6) while renewing our baptismal oaths to walk in its grace (Mt 3:13; Lk 22:20).[66] We experience the fellowship or *koinonia* of the Holy Spirit, not only with members of our local congregation but with believers in thousands of cultures around the world—and also with countless generations who have come before us who are already enjoying the fullness of the meal at Christ's heavenly table. At the table we find nourishment—like the ancient manna in the wilderness—to sustain us in our work and witness. And we experience a foretaste of the Lamb's wedding supper with his bride. The Lord's Supper reminds us that all of our activities—all of our practices—have a particular direction, aim, *telos*. The *telos* is the royal priesthood sharing fully in the joy and service taking place before God's throne in the fullness of the kingdom (Mt 25:10; Lk 22:16; Rev 19:7).

CONCLUSION: THE UNITY OF
WORSHIP, WORK AND WITNESS

How does the royal priesthood respond to God? We respond with worship, work and witness. We respond with the seven central practices of the royal priesthood: (1) baptism, (2) prayer, (3) *lectio divina* (divine reading), (4) ministry, (5) church discipline, (6) proclamation and (7) the Lord's Supper. While particular practices can be associated with particular persons of the triune God, ultimately our worship, work and witness are united when offered as spiritual sacrifices.

This ultimate unity is illustrated in the movie *Romero* (1989), which portrays the story of Salvadorian archbishop Oscar Romero. In one dramatic scene, Archbishop Romero is celebrating the Lord's Supper in a poverty-stricken pueblo deep in the country. The tiny town has been terrorized by government soldiers who have confiscated the local church for their headquarters, and the Archbishop has gone to lead the worship service as a sign of solidarity with the people. Soldiers interrupt the service and force the congregation to leave the building at gunpoint. Once outside, Archbishop Romero stops, turns and leads the congregation back into the church. The soldiers threaten to shoot, but the Archbishop ignores the guns, walks to the front of the church and leads the people in a celebration of the Lord's Supper as the soldiers stand and watch. As the Eucharist is celebrated, the Father receives *worship*, members of Christ's body experience the *work* of edification and the Holy Spirit is empowering *witness* to the world. While the Archbishop survives this scene of the movie, he was ultimately assassinated on March 24, 1980, while leading a different celebration of the Lord's Supper. His story is a reminder that faithful performances of the royal priesthood's seven practices will often lead to suffering. The biblical story of Daniel's commitment to prayer, even under pain of death, provides a similar example (Dan 6).

Archbishop Romero and Daniel remind us that covenant faithfulness to our baptismal vows is not an easy thing. Members of the royal priesthood face opposition from the flesh, the world and the devil. Our prayer is that once equipped with a clear vision of the royal priesthood's calling, with a firm intention to embrace this vision and with the means of the seven central practices, members of the royal priesthood and their local congregations will grow to be more like Christ—the great royal priest whose priesthood we share.

6

REPRESENTING CHRIST

Then one of the elders addressed me, saying, "Who are these, clothed in white robes, and from where have they come?" I said to him, "Sir, you know." And he said to me, "These are the ones coming out of the great tribulation. They have washed their robes and made them white in the blood of the Lamb.

"Therefore they are before the throne of God, and serve him day and night in his temple; and he who sits on the throne will shelter them with his presence."

REVELATION 7:13-15

ALL FOUR GOSPELS RECORD Jesus' saying "whoever would save his life will lose it, but whoever loses his life for my sake will find it" (Mk 8:35; Mt 10:39; Lk 9:24; Jn 12:25). These words provide another reminder of the powerful truth to which baptism points. Like Noah's flood, the waters that cover us symbolize the loss of our old life. As we rise from the water we publicly find our new life in Christ—a life of mission and ministry as members of Christ's royal priesthood. The life all baptized believers now live is one of royal and priestly service before the throne of God. We represent Christ to one another and to the world.

Christians in the Middle East understand that representing Christ is costly. In 2014 many Christians living in lands controlled by the Islamic State had their homes marked with the Arabic letter *nūn* (ن), which stands for "Nazarene." Believers who chose to represent Christ had their homes, businesses and churches spray-painted with the symbol. But many believers have faced much worse than the loss of home and property. Countless Middle Eastern believers have given their lives for their identification with Christ. In February of 2015 twenty-one Christians had their throats slit and were then decapitated because of their refusal to renounce Christ. Their mass martyrdom was displayed as a publicity video by the Islamic State. More powerful than the twenty-one black-robed executioners is the courage of the twenty-one Christian believers. Not one of the believers ran away or cried out in fear as they were led to martyrdom. Their last words, captured on the video, were *Ya Rabbi Yasou'* ("my Lord Jesus").

Milad Zaky, Abanub Atiya, Maged Shehata and the other eighteen Egyptian and African men martyred on that day understood that representing Christ is a serious calling. If the Western church hopes to faithfully perform the priesthood of all believers in our various contexts, we must take our privilege and responsibility no less seriously than our Middle Eastern brothers and sisters for whom baptism is a serious life and death commitment. Reclaiming the riches of the priesthood of all believers can help us in the Western church take our baptismal calling (or commission) just as seriously. Doing so may well bring suffering, but it will also bring great reward.

MATURE IN CHRIST, THE GREAT PRIEST-KING

This book has argued that Jesus the Christ (Anointed One) is the long-awaited Priest-King, the ruler of the beautiful and glorious city of God. The splendor of the heavenly Jerusalem is beyond description, but the hints we find in books such as Ezekiel and Revelation include images of light, gold, sparkling jewels, incredible trees, gardens, feasting and a joyful multitude of worshipers from every tongue, tribe and nation. This heavenly vision is not simply a futuristic vision—it has already begun. Disciples of Jesus participate in his royal priesthood in the present. This is our great privilege and responsibility. We share in Jesus' royal priesthood, and we represent him in the world.

Our desire in this book has been to paint a contemporary vision for representing Christ as members of his royal priesthood. Like Paul, our "labor" is to see each believer mature in Christ (Col 1:28-29). What separates the orthodox Christian doctrine of the priesthood of all believers from other versions is its absolute refusal to conceive of itself apart from the royal priesthood of Jesus Christ. A mature doctrine of the royal priesthood is Christocentric-Trinitarian. Through faith and the public proclamation of our baptisms we have been united to Christ, and we now share in his mission and ministry. Throughout the book we have explored this Christocentric vision of the priesthood of all believers through four perspectives. Next we take a few pages to review the ground we have covered.

ONE VISION, FOUR PERSPECTIVES

The Gospels present one Jesus, but he is seen from four different perspectives. Matthew, Mark, Luke and John each emphasizes and directs our attention to different aspects of Jesus' life and mission; reading them together gives us a fuller and more complete understanding of who Jesus is than reading any of them by themselves. In a similar way, this book has presented the doctrine of the priesthood of all believers from four perspectives: biblical, historical, theological and practical. Each perspective enriches our understanding and equips us to better appropriate the doctrine for our particular church contexts.

In the introduction we saw that the priesthood of all believers is a catholic doctrine. *Catholic* simply means "universal," or representative of all members of Christ's church. Every major branch of the church agrees with this doctrine, even if they may have lost sight of its importance at one time or another during the last two thousand years. The Orthodox church of the East knows the doctrine as "the priesthood of the baptized," the Roman Catholics as "the priesthood of the faithful" and the Protestant church as "the priesthood of all believers." All agree that that the doctrine is essential for a church to grow into maturity, into the "fullness of Christ" (Eph 4:13).

Biblical. The first perspective from which we approached the doctrine of the priesthood of all believers was that of biblical theology. Scripture is the authoritative tradition within the Great Tradition of the church.[1] All other perspectives must ultimately be judged against this norming norm. In the drama of God, the great protagonist is Jesus Christ, the Priest-King of Israel. It is Christ who has made an end of blood sacrifices through his sacrifice on the cross. Today his family of brothers and sisters share in his royal and priestly office by offering up spiritual sacrifices of praise and thanksgiving (Rom 12:1).

The people of God are a unified cast of performers, not a small caste of professionals with a great throng of spectators. All believers have a priestly ministry to fulfill. This priestly ministry can be fleshed out through study of the responsibilities of Levitical priests in the Old Testament. Members of the royal priesthood are called to discern, to teach, to judge, to read the Scriptures, to bless and to guard—all for the sake of the holiness of God's people. Within the royal priesthood some are ordained to leadership roles—but those in leadership are not more "priestly" than other members who hold forth the word of life (Phil 2:14-17).[2] Rather, each member of Christ's priestly body, the lowliest part as well as the most exalted, shares in Christ's royal priesthood. The transforming power of the doctrine of the priesthood of all believers is ultimately the way it helps believers grasp the great significance of our baptismal union with Christ.

The democratized royal priesthood of God's people is a major theme in Scripture. It helps believers understand connections between Adam and Eve in Eden and white-robed martyrs singing in the book of Revelation. It reveals connections between Exodus's royal priesthood and 1 Peter's priestly people, between Isaiah's promise of an end-time community made up of priests and ministers and Paul's claims about this same community in his many letters. The doctrine helps us to think with the author of Hebrews about the significance of the great royal Psalm 110, and it ultimately helps us understand more clearly the significance of many of the episodes recorded about Jesus in the four Gospels (e.g., the rent veil).

Historical. Our second perspective comes from the lens of history. It reveals that a proper understanding of the priesthood of all believers can release the transforming power of the church into the world in ways that shatter the status quo. Luther labored hard to help his generation understand that maturity in Christ meant embracing the privileges and responsibilities of the priesthood of all believers. There had been a gradual drift away from the doctrine over the previous twelve hundred years. Walls between ordained leaders and monastic orders on one hand and the rest of the priestly people of God on the other had grown to titanic heights. The vast majority of the baptized were not encouraged to know and proclaim God's Word, permitted to have the Scriptures in their common language or given access to the cup during the Lord's Supper.

Luther's great contribution to the church was the recovery of the priestly dignity of the whole people of God. His commitment to translate God's Word into the vernacular and his equipping of the whole people of God to teach God's Word to themselves and one another were the results. Luther's seven priestly functions of the whole people of God, described in his short booklet *Concerning the Ministry*, were revolutionary and provided a firm foundation for the ecclesial reforms he launched. Luther rediscovered and returned a priestly identity for the whole people of God. All God's people—the shoemaker and the milkmaid, the mother at home and the merchant in his shop—had a priestly vocation to represent Christ to one another and to seek the Father through the Son in prayer and in the Scriptures. Europe, and eventually the whole world, were powerfully influenced by this doctrine embodied in Luther's life and teaching. A faithful performance of the doctrine in our own century could release the same power in the church today.

Theological. Our third perspective for looking at the doctrine of the priesthood of all believers was theological. One mark of Christian maturity is a conscious awareness of a believer's distinct relationship with each member of the Trinity. A truly Christian doctrine of the royal priesthood will attend to the Father, the Son and the Holy Spirit. In chapter four we explored the dynamics of the relationship between the members of the royal priesthood and the triune God. We saw that the royal

priesthood can respond in especially appropriate ways to each
person of the Trinity. It is especially appropriate for the royal
priesthood to respond to the Father with worship and prayer; to
the Son with every-member ministry within Christ's temple-
body; to the Spirit with courageous witness in the world.

Focusing on one member of the Trinity does not mean the
others are ignored. Think again of Milad, Abanub, Maged and the
others martyred on a Libyan beach; they died with the words "my
Lord Jesus" on their lips. From where did the power for their courageous witness come? Or I think of Byron, a new believer at
church who began a Bible study at his high school in South Los
Angeles. Byron was repeatedly publicly mocked by one of his
teachers for identifying with Christ. Yet empowered by the Holy
Spirit, Byron continued to share the story of how Christ had transformed his life. The Egyptian martyrs and Byron all witnessed to
Christ, in the power of the Holy Spirit, for the glory of the Father.
Ultimately, the work of the triune God is undivided and so is the
response of the royal priesthood. But failing to attend to the triune
nature of the God the royal priesthood worships has resulted in a
number of inadequate versions of the doctrine—the most dangerous contemporary North American version being the "atomistic" distortion of the priesthood of all believers.

Practical. The final perspective from which we approached
the doctrine was practical. We strongly believe that Scripture is
a script to be performed, and the history of a doctrine can teach
us how our brothers and sisters have performed Scripture with
greater or lesser degrees of faithfulness in different cultural situations in the past.[3] Our job in the present is to learn from their
performances so that we can one day hear "Well done, my good
and faithful minister" from the great Priest-King. We are convinced that a faithful contemporary performance of the

priesthood of all believers will involve attention to seven practices. These are the same general practices identified by Luther: baptism, prayer, *lectio divina*, ministry, church discipline, proclamation and the Lord's Supper.

A long time ago a man named Noah received a *vision* for an ark. He decided (*intention*) to build it in the face of great opposition. God provided the *means*, and after one hundred years of labor an ark was built. Today's master builders working in the church will need to follow the same reliable VIM pattern: vision, intention and means. This book has sought to provide a vision from a variety of perspectives of what it might look like for the people of God to allow the doctrine of the priesthood of all believers to shape their identity and guide their practice. If the book stimulates you to deeper discussion and reflective action about how this doctrine might shape your life at home, at church and in the world, then we will deem the book a success.

So What?

In college I (Hank) attended a conference where after each plenary speaker finished, a woman would come to the platform and ask, "So what?" Twenty years later I can still hear her question ringing in my ears. So what? So what difference will this book make? So what will happen if our identity and imaginations are captured by a biblical vision of the royal priesthood? What kind of societal transformation would take place if all of the baptized began to take their priestly ministry seriously—in homes, hospitals, factories, investment banks, schools, technology companies, police departments, government, shops and, most importantly, churches? What if the church took its baptismal commissioning to share in the mission and ministry of Christ's royal priesthood seriously?

There are many possible answers to these questions. Luther's life illustrates the vast potential for transformation of church and world by a group highly committed to fleshing out the priesthood of baptized believers. We can imagine groups of parents or medical workers, groups of teachers or government professionals, groups of mechanics or social workers all meeting to reflect on what faithful priestly ministry looks like in their context. The priesthood of all believers has implications for the private life of the household, for the corporate life of the church and for believers' priestly witness in the world. As we saw in chapter four, Lesslie Newbigin thought this last aspect of the doctrine, what he called "the priesthood in the world," was what was most desperately needed in the West's post-Christendom context.

But again we ask, So what? So what if the priesthood of all believers is fleshed out in faithful ways at home, at church and in the world? What will be the result? The answer to this question can be found in an ancient scroll written more than 2,500 years ago. As we saw in chapter two, the main theme of the third part of Isaiah (Is 56–66) focuses on the servants of the Lord. This group is described as the "seed" of the Servant who will carry on his mission and ministry in the last days. At the heart of this larger section, what some commentators call the "theological core," is Isaiah 61 with its description of the servants as priests and ministers of the Lord (Is 61:6).[4]

This passage not only describes the followers of the suffering Servant as priestly, it also speaks about them wearing "a crown of beauty" (Is 61:3 NIV). The idea of God displaying his own beauty through his people is a central theme in the passage. The word for "beauty" appears some seven times in the immediate context. God will beautify his beautiful temple (Is 60:7). He will make his people beautiful (Is 60:9). He will beautify his sanctuary (Is 60:13). He will do all this so that he can display his beauty (Is 60:21). He will give his people a crown of beauty, a beautiful priestly crown (Is 61:3, 10). So what will happen if the royal priesthood takes Isaiah's vision of God's people as a royal priesthood seriously? The answer is simple—the beauty of God will be revealed in the world. The beauty of God's kingdom will be unveiled.

For the author of Isaiah 61, all this talk of beauty called to mind the image of a bride adorned with jewels (Is 61:10). A faithful performance of the royal priesthood will lead to greater displays of the Lamb's beauty on the face of his bride. That beauty of Christ will bring glory to the Father as it is displayed in sacrificial suffering and service on behalf of the world. The end has already begun. We now serve day and night before the throne in worship, work and witness. Like one of the first Christian songwriters, we too can sing, "I am a priest of the Lord, and I serve him as a priest."[5]

NOTES

CHAPTER 1: EXALTED CLERGY OR EGALITARIAN PRIESTS?

[1] Henri de Lubac, *The Splendor of the Church* (San Francisco: Ignatius, 1956), 27.

[2] See articles under Priest Sex Abuse Scandal, *The Huffington Post*, www.huffingtonpost.com/news/priest-sex-abuse-scandal; Michael Paulson, "Archbishop, Under Fire over Abuse, Apologizes but Says He Won't Resign," *New York Times*, July 30, 2014, www.nytimes.com/2014/07/31/us/archbishop-under-fire-over-abuse-apologizes-but-says-he-wont-resign.html; Nick Cumming-Bruce and Laurie Goodstein, "U.N. Panel Says Vatican Is Lax over Abusive Priests," *New York Times*, May 23, 2014, www.nytimes.com/2014/05/24/world/europe/vatican-fails-to-act-against-abusive-priests-panel-says.html.

[3] Victor Hugo, *Les Misérables* (New York: Random House, 2008), 5-6.

[4] Ibid., 89-90.

[5] Jane Austen, *Pride and Prejudice*, ed. Joseph Pearce (San Francisco: Ignatius, 2008), 73.

[6] For example, see Stephen Rowland, "Splitting Hairs," *The Daily Herald*, February 23, 2012, http://columbiadailyherald.com/sections/lifestyles/religion/splitting-hairs.html.

[7] Paul, however, does refer to himself as a "minister" (*leitourgon*) of Christ and to his proclamation of the gospel and the offering of the Gentiles as a "priestly" (*ierourgounta*) service to God (Rom 15:16).

[8]Much of the subsequent discussion draws on Colin Bulley, *The Priesthood of Some Believers: Developments from the General to the Special Priesthood in the Christian Literature of the First Three Centuries*, Paternoster Biblical and Theological Monographs (Waynesboro, GA: Paternoster, 2000), and Cyril Eastwood, *The Royal Priesthood of the Faithful: An Investigation of the Doctrine from Biblical Times to the Reformation* (Minneapolis: Augsburg, 1963).

[9]Eastwood, *Royal Priesthood*, 62-66.

[10]Origen, *Homilies on Leviticus: 1–16*, trans. Gary Barkley, FC 83 (Washington, DC: Catholic University of America Press, 1990), 4.6.2 (78); 4.6.5 (79); 5.12.9 (115); 6.2.3 (118); 6.2.6 (119); 6.5.6 (119), where all believers are called "high priests"; 9.1.3 (177); 9.9.3 (196); 9.9.3 (x2, 196); 9.9.4 (197); 9.9.6 (198); and 13.5.4 (243), which emphasizes that "all we who believe in Christ are now a priestly race" (authors' translation).

[11]For an encyclopedic list see Paul Dabin, *Le Sacerdoce Royal Des Fidèles Dans la Tradicion Ancienne et Moderne* (Paris: L'Edition Universelle, 1950), 69-258.

[12]Nicholas Afanasiev, *The Church of the Holy Spirit*, ed. Michael Plekon, trans. Vitaly Permiakov (Notre Dame, IN: University of Notre Dame Press, 2007), 25-26.

[13]Sebastian Brock, "The Priesthood of the Baptized: Some Syriac Perspectives," *Sobornost* 9 (1987): 15.

[14]John D. Zizioulas, *Being as Communion: Studies in Personhood and the Church* (Crestwood, NY: St. Vladimir's Seminary, 1985), 215-16 (emphases original).

[15]It should be noted that the "priesthood of the baptized" is also commonly used in the Roman Catholic tradition, and both Luther and Barth emphasized the relationship between baptism and the public ordination of believers to the ministry of the royal priesthood.

[16]David Orr, "The Giving of the Priesthood to the Faithful," in *Priesthood: The Hard Questions*, ed. Gerald Gleeson (Newtown, Australia: Downer, 1993), 72.

[17]Oscar A. Romero, *The Violence of Love*, trans. James R. Brockman (Maryknoll, NY: Orbis Books, 2004), 24.

[18]*Catechism of the Catholic Church* (New York: Doubleday, 1995), 430.

[19]Ibid., 431.

[20]See discussion in Hans Küng, *The Church*, trans. Ray and Rosaleen Ock-
enden (New York: Sheed and Ward, 1967), 363-87; Gerald O'Collins and
Michael Keenan Jones, *Jesus Our Priest: A Christian Approach to the
Priesthood of Christ* (Oxford: Oxford University Press, 2010), 272-93.

[21]Daniel Liechty, ed., *Early Anabaptist Spirituality: Selected Writings*
(Mahwah, NJ: Paulist, 1994), 9.

[22]Franklin H. Littell, "The Radical Reformation," in *The Layman in
Christian History: A Project of the Department on the Laity of the World
Council of Churches*, ed. Stephen C. Neill and Hans Ruedi Weber (Phila-
delphia: Westminster, 1963), 270.

Chapter 2: A Royal Priesthood

[1]John Elliott, *The Elect and the Holy: An Exegetical Examination of 1 Peter
2:4-10 and the Phrase* Basileion Hierateuma, NovTSup (Leiden: Brill,
1966), xiii-xiv.

[2]Elliott, *Elect and the Holy*, 174.

[3]Although it has been pointed out that each of the two terms has a different
nuance, they also exhibit semantic overlap that makes it difficult to determine any substantial difference from the context. For a brief but helpful
discussion of these terms, see J. Richard Middleton, *The Liberating Image:
The* Imago Dei *in Genesis 1* (Grand Rapids: Brazos, 2005), 45-48.

[4]Middleton, *Liberating Image*, 51. Lohfink points out other non-royal uses
of *rada*, but these still have a connotation of one's rule over another or
dominance over something. See Norbert Lohfink, "'Subdue the Earth?'
(Genesis 1:28)," in *Theology of the Pentateuch: Themes of the Priestly Narrative and Deuteronomy*, trans. Linda M. Maloney (Minneapolis: Fortress, 1994), 11-12.

[5]James Limburg says rightly: "Thus when Gen 1 speaks about human
beings exercising dominion over the earth and its creatures, the language
is drawn from the sphere of politics and the exercise of kingship as it
ought to be. This ideal model for the relationship between humankind
(man and woman) and the earth and its creatures is the king/people relationship." James Limburg, "The Responsibility of Royalty: Genesis 1–11
and the Care of the Earth," *Word and World* 11 (1991): 126.

[6]See Middleton, *Liberating Image*, 53-54.

[7]D. J. A. Clines, "The Image of God in Man," *Tyndale Bulletin* 19 (1968): 97.

[8]The Ancient Near East background to the phrase "image of God" suggests that it would have communicated two main ideas: the sonship and rulership of the king. The monarch is the image of god in that he has a special relationship to the god as son and to the world as ruler for the deity. Gentry examines Egyptian notions of the king as the son of the gods. Sonship and image are not about physical resemblance but about reflecting the essential behavior of the god. Therefore image and sonship denote the "essential notions of the god." In Egyptian culture, the king is the "living statue of the god" and represents the deity on earth through rule and conquest. Peter J. Gentry, "Kingdom Through Covenant: Humanity as the Divine Image," *Southern Baptist Journal of Theology* 12 (2008): 27. Here Gentry summarizes the more thorough work of Dion, who also examines Mesopotamian parallels: Paul E. Dion, "Ressemblance et Image de Dieu: Égypte et Mésopotamie," in *Supplément au Dictionnaire de la Bible*, ed. L. Pirot and A. Robert (Paris: Letouzey & Ané, 1985), 10:366-75. Cf. Clines, "Image of God in Man," 70-85. This connection between sonship and the divine image is also found in Genesis 5:1-3, where the idea that Adam had a son "in his own likeness" is analogous to God creating Adam in his likeness.

[9]Middleton, *Liberated Image*, 88.

[10]Humankind's dignity is highlighted in Psalm 8, which many view as a commentary on Genesis 1:26-31. Although the psalm does not employ the exact language of image, likeness or rule, it speaks of humanity as "crowned" with "glory and honor" (8:5)—likely royal references—and as having "dominion" over all the creatures of the earth (8:6-8).

[11]For example, see Margaret Barker, *The Gate of Heaven: The History and Symbolism of the Temple in Jerusalem* (London: SPCK, 1991); G. K. Beale, *The Temple and the Church's Mission: A Biblical Theology of the Dwelling Place of God* (Downers Grove, IL: IVP Academic, 2004); William J. Dumbrell, *The Search for Order: Biblical Eschatology in Focus* (Grand Rapids: Baker, 1994), 24-25; Meredith G. Kline, *Images of the Spirit* (Grand Rapids: Baker, 1980), 35-47; John H. Walton, *Genesis*, NIVAC (Grand Rapids: Zondervan, 2001), 172-74; John H. Walton, *The Lost World of Genesis One: Ancient Cosmology and the Origins Debate* (Downers Grove, IL: IVP Academic, 2009), 72-92; Gordon J. Wenham, "Sanctuary Symbolism in the Garden of Eden Story," in *I Studied Inscriptions from Before the Flood: Ancient Near Eastern, Literary, and Linguistic*

Approaches to Genesis 1–11, ed. Richard S. Hess and David Toshio Tsumura (Winona Lakes, IN: Eisenbrauns, 1994), 399-406.

[12]Among the signs are the facts that (1) the garden is the unique dwelling for God's presence, (2) the tree of life is represented by the temple's golden lampstand, (3) the golden cherubim guarding the ark of the covenant reflect the first guarding cherubim in Eden, (4) extensive garden imagery appears in Israel's temple, (5) both garden and temple have east-facing entrances, (6) Ezekiel (Ezek 28:13-18) and early Judaism depict the garden as the first sanctuary and (7) some ANE temples had garden-like features (Beale, *Temple and the Church's Mission*, 66-80). For Beale's more recent and popular work, see G. K. Beale and Mitchell Kim, *God Dwells Among Us: Expanding Eden to the Ends of the Earth* (Downers Grove, IL: InterVarsity Press, 2014), chapters 1–2. Also see John H. Walton, *The Lost World of Adam and Eve: Genesis 2–3 and the Human Origins Debate* (Downers Grove, IL: IVP Academic, 2015), 104-15.

[13]Beale, *Temple and the Church's Mission*, 66-67. Wenham adds that *dbu* refers to the Levites' guarding of the tabernacle from intruders (Num 1:53; 3:7-8). Gordon J. Wenham, *Genesis 1–15*, WBC 1 (Waco, TX: Word, 1987), 67.

[14]Targums Neofiti and Pseudo-Jonathan on Genesis 2:15 call attention to Adam's priestly role when they render his function as "to toil in the Law and to observe its commandments." Adam is elsewhere presented as being created at the location of the temple (Tg. Pseudo-Jonathan Gen 3:23) and from the dust of the sanctuary site (Tg. Pseudo-Jonathan Gen 2:7), and as using sanctuary language in naming the animals (Tg. Neofiti Gen 2:19). See Beale, *Temple and the Church's Mission*, 67.

[15]Wenham, "Sanctuary Symbolism," 401-2.

[16]Beale, *Temple and the Church's Mission*, 68. Also see Walton, *Genesis*, 173, for a nearly identical conclusion.

[17]Sebastian Brock, "The Priesthood of the Baptized: Some Syriac Perspectives," *Sobornost* 9 (1987): 16-18.

[18]See Beale, *Temple and the Church's Mission*, 69.

[19]I am in agreement with those who hold that the character of the tree is of little interest in the story. The main issue is the fact of the command and the authority of the one giving it. See Walter Brueggemann, *Genesis*, IBC (Atlanta: John Knox, 1982), 46.

[20]Ibid., 46.

[21]See Beale and Kim, *God Dwells Among Us*, 29-38.

[22]See Beale, *Temple and the Church's Mission*, particularly the whole of chapter 3 for a summary of the argument.

[23]Beale, *Temple and the Church's Mission*, 83. Dumbrell suggests that Genesis 1 emphasizes humankind's kingship while Genesis 2 stresses Adam's priesthood (Dumbrell, *Search for Order*, 25). However, if our connecting of the two passages is correct then both duties/offices are emphasized in each passage. Walton maintains that in Egypt the preservation of order in the sacred space from the chaotic forces of the cosmos was typically a task for both priest and king. If the thinking is similar in Genesis, then this combines the subduing and ruling of chapter 1 with the serving/cultivating and keeping/guarding of chapter 2 (Walton, *Genesis*, 173-74). Cf. Terence E. Fretheim, "Genesis," in *The New Interpreters Bible*, vol. 1 (Nashville, TN: Abingdon, 1994), 351.

[24]Beale, *Temple and the Church's Mission*, 82. Barker describes the garden (and other Israelite sanctuaries) as that which controls and drives back the threatening and chaotic forces of evil. In ancient Israelite thought, she notes, temples were "the centre of the created world and the key to its wellbeing" (Barker, *Gate of Heaven*, 19, 57).

[25]The connection between the proclamation of Yahweh and his word and royal priesthood becomes clearer in later canonical literature.

[26]John A. Davies, *A Royal Priesthood: Literary and Intertextual Perspectives on an Image of Israel in Exodus 19:6*, JSOTSup 395 (London: T&T Clark, 2004), 43.

[27]Patrick paraphrases the conditional sentence: "Being Yahweh's own possession, his holy nation and kingdom of priests, entails submitting to his will." Dale Patrick, "The Covenant Code Source," *VT* 27 (1977): 145-57. Cf. Deut 7:6-11; 26:18-19.

[28]For a helpful presentation of the main interpretations of the title, see Davies, *Royal Priesthood*, 70-86.

[29]Ibid., 89.

[30]Nahum Sarna, *Exodus*, JPSTC (New York: Jewish Publication Society, 1991), 104.

[31]Leopold Sabourin, *Priesthood: A Comparative Study*, SHR 25 (Leiden: Brill, 1973), 98-99.

[32]Davies, *Royal Priesthood*, 164.

[33]Ibid., 166.

[34]Gottlob Schrenk, "hiereus," in *Theological Dictionary of the New Testament*, ed. Gerhard Kittel and Geoffrey W. Bromiley, trans. Geoffrey W. Bromiley (Grand Rapids: Eerdmans, 1965), 3:260.

[35]T. F. Torrance, *Royal Priesthood*, Scottish Journal of Theology Occasional Papers 3 (London: Oliver and Boyd, 1955), 1.

[36]This would also pertain to the "guarding and serving" mentioned earlier in reference to Adam's priesthood. However, our focus is on those practices that would prove important for understanding the priesthood of believers.

[37]On the tabernacle, see Leviticus 10:1-10; Numbers 3:5-10; 18:1-7; on sabbath and holy days, see Exodus 34:18; Leviticus 26:2; Deuteronomy 5:12-15; on guarding covenant, see Exodus 32:25-29.

[38]"The making of distinctions is the essence of the priestly function." Jacob Milgrom, *Leviticus 1–16: A New Translation with Introduction and Commentary*, AB 3 (New Haven, CT: Yale University Press, 1998), 615. In Ezekiel 22:26 we see an example of the priestly failure to perform their duty, allowing profane objects to be used for the worship of Yahweh. This neglect perpetuated the defilement of God's people and received the condemnation of God.

[39]J. G. McConville, *Deuteronomy*, AOTC 5 (Downers Grove, IL: IVP Academic, 2002), 291.

[40]See, e.g., Philip J. Budd, *Numbers*, WBC 5 (Waco, TX: Word, 1984), 76; Rolf P. Knierim and George W. Coats, *Numbers*, FOTL 4 (Grand Rapids: Eerdmans, 2005), 94; Jacob Milgrom, *Numbers*, JPSTC (Philadelphia: The Jewish Publication Society, 1990), 51.

[41]Budd, *Numbers*, 77.

[42]David Hay, *Glory at the Right Hand: Psalm 110 in Early Christianity* (Nashville, TN: Abingdon, 1973), 15, 163-66.

[43]The parenthetical translation is taken from John Goldingay, *Psalms*, vol. 3, *Psalms 90–150*, Baker Commentary of the Old Testament Wisdom and Psalms (Grand Rapids: Baker Academic, 2008), 296.

[44]Leslie C. Allen, *Psalms 110–150*, WBC 21 (Waco, TX: Word, 1983), 81.

[45]Ibid., 82. Goldingay notes that Israelite kings performed priestly functions, such as leading worship and prayer, but likely did not offer sacrifices as a norm (Goldingay, *Psalms*, 3:296).

[46]See, for example, Oscar Cullman, *The Christology of the New Testament*, trans. Shirley C. Guthrie and Charles A. M. Hall (Philadelphia: Westminster John Knox, 1959), 83, 91-92; Daniel Block, "My Servant David:

Ancient Israel's Vision of the Messiah," in *Israel's Messiah in the Bible and the Dead Sea Scrolls* (Grand Rapids: Baker, 2003), 17-56; J. A. Motyer, *The Prophecy of Isaiah: An Introduction and Commentary* (Downers Grove, IL: InterVarsity Press, 1993), 13-16.

[47] For an important treatment of the priestly "seed" of the Servant, see W. A. M. Beuken, "The Main Theme of Trito-Isaiah, 'The Servants of Yhwh,'" *Journal for the Study of the Old Testament* 47 (1990): 67-87.

[48] John N. Oswalt, *The Book of Isaiah: Chapters 40–66*, NICOT, (Grand Rapids: Eerdmans, 1998), 571-72.

[49] Ibid., 572.

[50] Ibid., 564. Also see Motyer, *Isaiah*, 493; Joseph Blenkinsopp, *Isaiah 56–66*, AB 19B (New York: Doubleday, 2003), 201.

[51] Motyer, *Isaiah*, 493; Marten H. Woudstra, *The Book of Joshua*, NICOT (Grand Rapids: Eerdmans, 1981), 63.

[52] See Motyer, *Isaiah*, 493; Oswalt, *Isaiah 40–66*, 564.

[53] Peter J. Leithart, *The Priesthood of the Plebs: A Theology of Baptism* (Eugene, OR: Wipf & Stock, 2003), 95.

[54] Ibid., 112.

[55] Hebrews 5:5-8 pairs Psalm 2 and Psalm 110 in order to show that Jesus is Jerusalem's high-priestly King. Hebrews makes extensive use of this pairing. The introductory exordium (Heb 1:1-4) alludes to Psalms 2:7 and 110:4, and Hebrews 1:5-13 uses Psalms 2:7 and 110:1 as bookends in a string of seven Old Testament quotations.

[56] John's Gospel could have been included, as it contains a few implicit references to Jesus' priesthood. For example, during Jesus' trial before the high priest he is questioned about his disciples and teaching (Jn 18:19). Jesus responds that he has taught the Jews openly in the temple and synagogues, not taking secret counsel like the high priest and his companions.

[57] Edwin K. Broadhead, "Christology as Polemic and Apologetic: The Priestly Portrait of Jesus in the Gospel of Mark," *JSNT* 47 (1992): 24-25; cf. Robert A. Guelich, *Mark 1–8:26*, WBC 34A (Dallas: Word, 1989), 77.

[58] Crispin H. T. Fletcher-Louis, "Jesus as the High Priestly Messiah: Part 2," *JSHJ* 5 (2007): 64-66; cf. Guelich, *Mark*, 74.

[59] Fletcher-Louis, "Jesus as the High Priestly Messiah: Part 2," 66-69.

[60] See ibid., 75-77. Cf. Broadhead, "Christology as Polemic," 28.

[61] Broadhead, "Christology as Polemic," 28.

[62]Ibid., 28-29.

[63]It is also noteworthy that Jesus is declared the "Holy One of God" (Mk 1:24), a title whose human precedent can only be found in Aaron (Num 16:7; Ps 106:16). See Fletcher-Louis, "Jesus as the High Priestly Messiah: Part 2," 63.

[64]Similarities between John and Jesus include announcement scenes to Zechariah and Mary (Lk 1:5-38), their "songs" (Lk 1:46-55, 67-79), stories of circumcision and naming (Lk 1:59-63; 2:21), descriptions of both boys growing up (Lk 1:80; 2:40, 52) and the fact that they were both teachers of Israel (Lk 3:18; 19:47-48). There are also similarities to the early life of Samuel that intimate a parallel calling and ministry—that is, to raise up a faithful priest (1 Sam 2:35). Leithart, *Priesthood*, 114-15.

[65]Ibid., 119-20. Some scholars view this incident as pointing to Jesus as the eschatological Prophet. However, a priestly reading seems more likely in light of the Aaronic and tabernacle/temple imagery throughout this passage.

[66]Ibid., 120. The fact that the temple features prominently in the early and latter chapters of Luke is further (implicit) evidence of Luke's presentation of Jesus as priest. For example, when Jesus is twelve he is found in the temple, sitting among the teachers, reasoning about the law and amazing his listeners by his wisdom and understanding (Lk 2:46-47). The image of the Holy Spirit overshadowing Mary (Lk 1:35) alludes to the descent of glory on the Mosaic tabernacle (Ex 40:34-35) (ibid., 112-13).

[67]Otto Betz, "Jesus and Isaiah 53," in *Jesus and the Suffering Servant: Isaiah 53 and Christian Origins*, ed. W. H. Bellinger and William Reuben Farmer (Harrisburg, PA: Trinity Press International, 1998), 86.

[68]See, for example, Daniel Gurtner, *The Torn Veil: Matthew's Exposition of the Death of Jesus* (Cambridge: Cambridge University Press, 2007), 2-28; Donald Hagner, *Matthew 14–28*, WBC 33B (Dallas: Word, 1995), 849; Ulrich Luz, *Matthew: A Commentary*, Continental Commentaries (Minneapolis: Augsburg Fortress, 1989), 3:595-96.

[69]O'Collins and Jones make the point that if the apostle Paul's preaching can be described as priestly (Rom 15:16), then Jesus' preaching should be even more so. Gerald O'Collins and Michael Keenan Jones, *Jesus Our Priest: A Christian Approach to the Priesthood of Christ* (Oxford: Oxford University Press, 2010), 16.

[70]Paul J. Achtemeier, *1 Peter: A Commentary on First Peter*, Hermeneia (Minneapolis: Fortress, 1996), 154.

[71]Thomas R. Schreiner, *1, 2 Peter, Jude*, NAC 37 (Nashville, TN: Broadman & Holman, 2003), 105.

[72]Achtemeier, *1 Peter*, 155; John H. Elliott, *1 Peter: A New Translation with Introduction and Commentary*, AB 37B (New York: Doubleday, 2000), 414-18.

[73]Elliott, *1 Peter*, 420.

[74]Ibid., 422; Elliott, *Elect and the Holy*, 197; Leonhard Goppelt, *A Commentary on I Peter*, ed. Ferdinand Hahn, trans. John E. Alsup (Grand Rapids: Eerdmans, 1993), 142; Schreiner, *1, 2 Peter, Jude*, 107.

[75]Karen H. Jobes, *1 Peter*, BECNT (Grand Rapids: Baker Academic, 2005), 151.

[76]Ibid., 163.

[77]Schreiner, *1, 2 Peter, Jude*, 116; cf. Elliot, *Elect and the Holy*, 197. Those who see only reference to worship here include J. Ramsey Michaels, *1 Peter*, WBC 49 (Waco, TX: Word, 1988), 110.

[78]Ernest Best, "Spiritual Sacrifice: General Priesthood in the New Testament," *Interpretation* 14 (1960): 287.

[79]Morris observes that *dokimazein* contains elements of "testing" and doing, since what Paul has in mind is not just the knowing of God's will but the performance of it. Leon Morris, *The Epistle to the Romans*, PNTC (Grand Rapids: Eerdmans, 1988), 436.

[80]See Douglas Moo, *The Epistle to the Romans*, NICNT (Grand Rapids: Eerdmans, 1996), 889-90. Cf. Thomas R. Schreiner, *Romans*, BECNT 6 (Grand Rapids: Baker Academic, 1998), 766.

[81]Schreiner, *Romans*, 767.

[82]David Peterson, *Engaging with God: A Biblical Theology of Worship* (Downers Grove, IL: InterVarsity Press, 1992), 181-82.

[83]Gordon D. Fee, *Paul's Letter to the Philippians*, NICNT (Grand Rapids: Eerdmans, 1995), 251.

[84]See Moisés Silva, *Philippians*, 2nd ed., BECNT (Grand Rapids: Baker, 2008), 129.

[85]As James Ware notes, "The Philippians' identity as priests also reflects Paul's conviction that the eschatological time of renewal had dawned in Christ Jesus. . . . Paul's use of this imagery thus depicts the Philippians as priests to the surrounding pagan world." James Ware, *The Mission of the Church in Paul's Letter to the Philippians in the Context of Ancient Judaism* (Boston: Brill, 2005), 273.

[86]For an extensive argument for why drawing near in this context refers to prayer, see John M. Scholer, *Proleptic Priests: Priesthood in the Epistle to the Hebrews*, JSNTSup 49 (Sheffield: Sheffield Academic, 1991), 107-12. Cf. William L. Lane, *Hebrews 1–8*, WBC 47A (Dallas: Word, 1991), 115.

[87]For an in-depth study of the use of *proserchomai* in the Septuagint and Hebrews, see Scholer, *Proleptic Priests*, 91-149.

[88]Brooke Foss Westcott, *The Epistle to the Hebrews* (Grand Rapids: Eerdmans, 1950), 108.

[89]For arguments regarding the priestly consecration and Christian baptism parallel, see Leithart, *Priesthood of the Plebs*, 100-102.

[90]See Lambertus Floor, "The General Priesthood of Believers in the Epistle to the Hebrews," in *Ad Hebraeos: Essays on the Epistle to the Hebrews* (Pretoria: Die Nuwe-Testamentiese Werkgemeenskap van Suid-Afrika, 1971), 76-80.

[91]Lane, *Hebrews 1–8*, 288.

[92]Samuel Bénétreau, *L'Épitre aux Hebreux*, vol. 2, CEB (Paris: Edifac, 1990), 227; cf. Floor, "General Priesthood," 78.

[93]Other passages in Hebrews could have been surveyed. For example, Hebrews 7:19, 25; 11:6; 12:18-24 (see Scholer, *Proleptic Priests*, 113-48).

[94]G. K. Beale, *The Book of Revelation*, NIGTC (Grand Rapids: Eerdmans, 1999), 194-96.

[95]Ibid., 361.

[96]Apart from these explicit references to kingship and priesthood, priestly themes occur throughout the book (e.g., Rev 7:15; 22:3, where the saints "serve" God). Grant R. Osborne, *Revelation*, BECNT (Grand Rapids: Baker, 2002), 709.

[97]It is also possible that the reference to overcoming believers as pillars in God's temple (Rev 3:12) has priestly connotations, as these people, like priests, will become permanent fixtures in God's house. In chapters 21 and 22 believers are depicted as permanent fixtures in the new Jerusalem temple-city.

[98]Beale, *Revelation*, 193.

[99]Yves Congar, "The Different Priesthoods: Christian, Jewish, and Pagan," in *A Gospel Priesthood*, trans. P. F. Hepburne-Scott (New York: Herder and Herder, 1967), 75.

Chapter 3: Priesthood Reformed

[1]Martin Luther, *The Freedom of the Christian* (1520), in *Luther's Works*, ed. Jaroslav Pelikan and Helmut T. Lehmann (St. Louis and Philadelphia: Fortress Press, 1955–1986), 31:352. Further citations from Luther refer to volumes in *Luther's Works* (*LW*).

[2]Ibid., *LW* 31:354.

[3]Timothy J. Wengert, *Priesthood, Pastors, Bishops: Public Ministry for the Reformation and Today* (Minneapolis: Fortress, 2008), 1, 6.

[4]The most comprehensive study of the royal priesthood of the faithful demonstrates the non-novelty of Luther's ideas concerning the priesthood of believers. See Paul Dabin, *Le Sacerdoce Royal des Fidèles dans la Tradicion Ancienne et Moderne* (Paris: L'Edition Universelle, 1950). Similarly, see Colin Bulley, *The Priesthood of Some Believers: Developments from the General to the Special Priesthood in the Christian Literature of the First Three Centuries* (Waynesboro, GA: Paternoster, 2000) for a study of the doctrine in the early patristic period.

[5]Tertullian, *On Baptism* 17, *The Ante-Nicene Fathers*, 3:677.

[6]Tertullian, *The Prescription Against Heretics* 41 (Ante-Nicene Fathers 3:263).

[7]Bulley, *Priesthood of Some Believers*, 78-85, 137.

[8]Ray Noll highlights another early development leading to the sacralization of Christian ministry: "The first step in this development . . . appears to have been the emergence of a single bishop (*monepískopos*) at various places in the Mediterranean world supplanting the earlier charismatic and then committee forms of church order along with a parallel development of sacral-cultic language and attitudes whereby the people gradually begin to see their *monepískopos*, their primary liturgical officer, as a 'high priest' (*archiereús*) representing Jesus Christ, the High Priest." Ray Robert Noll, *Christian Ministerial Priesthood: A Search for Its Beginnings in the Primary Documents of the Apostolic Fathers* (San Francisco: Catholic Scholars Press, 1993), 3.

[9]Of Cyprian, one author writes: "Despite the obvious contrasts, the Eucharist and its ministers were for him direct successors of the cultus and priesthood of the Jerusalem temple, and also superior equivalents to the demonic gentile sacrifices still being offered in their own city." Andrew B. McGowan, *Ancient Christian Worship: Early Church Practices in Social, Historical, and*

Theological Perspective (Grand Rapids: Baker Academic, 2014), 54. Also see Alister C. Stewart, *The Original Bishops: Office and Order in the First Christian Communities* (Grand Rapids: Baker Academic, 2014) for an account of the Jewish origins of church offices in the early church.

[10] Cyril Eastwood, *The Royal Priesthood of the Faithful: An Investigation of the Doctrine from Biblical Times to the Reformation* (Eugene, OR: Wipf & Stock, 2009), 81-82.

[11] "Unity" here and throughout refers to "Catholic Unity," an "exclusive doctrine encased in an unalterable form" to which all must subscribe in order to truly be in the church. Ibid., 82.

[12] Ibid., 83.

[13] Ibid. Cyprian writes: "They are the Church who are a people united to the priest and the flock which adheres to their pastor. Whence you ought to know that the bishop is in the Church, and the Church in the bishop; and if any one be not with the bishop, that he is not in the Church, and that those flatter themselves in vain who creep in, not having peace with God's priests.... The Church ... is indeed connected and bound together by the cement of priests who cohere with one another." Cyprian, *Epistle* 68.8 (ANF 5:374-75).

[14] Eastwood, *Royal Priesthood*, 84-85.

[15] Ibid., 85-87.

[16] McGowan, *Ancient Christian Worship*, 159.

[17] An ordination prayer of Hippolytus: "Now through the mediation of your Christ pour forth through us the power of your princely Spirit which was at the service of your beloved child Jesus Christ, which was given by your will to the holy apostles of you, the eternal God. Grant in your name ... to this your servant ... to feed your holy flock and to exercise the high priesthood for you, blamelessly serving night and day and propitiating your countenance; to gather the number of those being saved, and to offer the gifts of your holy Church. Grant to him, almighty Lord, through your Christ the fellowship of the Holy Spirit, so that he may have power to forgive sins, ... to loose every bond, ... to please you ... in offering a pure and bloodless sacrifice which you instituted through Christ." Hippolytus, *Apostolic Constitutions* 8.5, in Paul F. Bradshaw, *Ordination Rites of the Ancient Churches of East and West* (New York: Pueblo, 1990), 114. Cf. Everett Ferguson, "Ordination," in *Encyclopedia of Early Christianity*, ed. Everett Ferguson, 2nd ed. (New York: Garland, 1997), 2:833.

[18]Augustine continues: "For neither sacrament may be wronged. If a sacrament necessarily becomes void in the case of the wicked, both must become void; if it remain valid with the wicked, this must be so with both. If, therefore, the baptism be acknowledged which he could not lose who severed himself from the unity of the Church, that baptism must also be acknowledged which was administered by one who by his secession had not lost the sacrament of conferring baptism." Augustine, *On Baptism, Against the Donatists* 1.1.2 (*NPNF*[1] 4:412).

[19]Ibid. (emphasis added).

[20]Thomas M. Finn, "Anointing," in *Encyclopedia of Early Christianity*, ed. Everett Ferguson, 2nd ed. (New York: Garland, 1999), 1:57. Cf. Leonel L. Mitchell, *Baptismal Anointing* (Notre Dame, IN: University of Notre Dame, 1978), 60-70.

[21]The anointing of the head furthermore signified the move from mere presbyter to supreme pontiff. Antonio Santantoni, "Ordination and Ministries in the West," in *Handbook for Liturgical Studies: Sacraments and Sacramentals*, ed. Anscar J. Chupungco (Collegeville, MN: Liturgical Press, 2000), 231-32.

[22]Leithart, *Priesthood of the Plebs*, 227.

[23]Gelasius I, "Letter to the Emperor Anastasius," in Brian Tierney, *The Crisis of Church & State 1050–1300* (Englewood Cliffs, NJ: Prentice-Hall, 1964), 13-14.

[24]During which time, measures were taken to strengthen the clergy's power to select the pope. John A. F. Thomson, *The Western Church in the Middle Ages* (London: Arnold, 1998), 83.

[25]Thomson, *Western Church*, 85-87. Of course, the emphasis on celibacy may have been motivated by other reasons beyond purity, such as the prevention of clerical dynasties. For a discussion of the issues at the time of Gregory's reform, see Helen L. Parish, *Clerical Celibacy in the West, c. 1100–1700* (Burlington, VA: Ashgate, 2010), 87-122.

[26]Uta-Renate Blumenthal, *The Investiture Controversy: Church and Monarchy from the Ninth to the Twelfth Century* (Philadelphia: University of Pennsylvania Press, 1988), 34.

[27]Gregory VII, "Decrees Against Lay Investiture," in Tierney, *Crisis of Church and State*, 51-52 (emphasis added).

[28]Leithart, *Priesthood of the Plebs*, 232-33.

[29]Eugene IV, "Decree for the Armenians (*Exultate Deo*)," in *The Sources of Catholic Dogma*, ed. Henry Denzinger, trans. Roy J. Deferrari (St. Louis: B. Herder, 1957), 221. The Council of Trent merely upheld this traditional understanding of the priesthood and sacrament of orders. In the Canons on the Sacrament of Order we read, "If anyone says that by sacred ordination the Holy Spirit is not imparted, and that therefore the bishops say in vain: 'Receive ye the Holy Spirit'; or that by it a character is not imprinted or that he who has once been a priest can again become a layman: let him be anathema." Council of Trent, Session XXIII, July 15, 1563, in Denzinger, *Sources of Catholic Dogma*, 295.

[30]This view was indicative of a general Realist view of the world, where the church stood as the intermediary in a hierarchy consisting of God above and humanity below. See Steven E. Ozment, *The Age of Reform, 1250–1550: An Intellectual and Religious History of Late Medieval and Reformation Europe* (New Haven, CT: Yale University Press, 1980), 62-63.

[31]Gounelle lists four criticisms of the Roman priesthood that underlie Luther's doctrine of universal priesthood: (1) a mediation between God and believers other than that of Jesus Christ, (2) the necessity of the ministry, (3) the idea of a sacrifice offered to God in the Eucharist and (4) the notion that the clergy have a "character" different than the laity. It is the last of these that is most relevant to this study. André Gounelle, "Le sacerdoce universel," Études *Théologiques et Religieuses* 63 (1988): 429-32. It might also be noted (and this is suggested in Gounelle's list) that Luther had "political" motivations for opposing the current state of priesthood.

[32]*Estate* is an older term meaning "walk of life" or "standing." Wengert, *Priesthood*, 5.

[33]Luther's opponents and therefore the target of his polemics changed throughout his career. Prior to 1525 he focused on the elevation of clergy over laity (the Roman Church), while after 1525 he fought against radicals who denied the importance of clergy. Herman A. Preus, "Luther and the Universal Priesthood and the Office of the Ministry," *Concordia Journal* 5 (1979): 55. Luther also rejected the sacrament of orders because, in his opinion, it was behind many clerical abuses. I will not treat this concern of Luther's here. See, for example, *Against the Spiritual Estate of the Pope* (1522), *LW* 39:270-99; *To the Christian Nobility of the German Nation Concerning the Reform of the Christian Estate* (1520), *LW* 44:142.

[34]Martin Luther, *The Babylonian Captivity of the Church* (1520), *LW* 36:106-7.

[35]Rome, however, argued on the basis of Hebrews 7:12 ("when there is a change in the priesthood, there is necessarily a change in the law") that it had the right to make new laws. Luther refutes this claim in *The Misuse of the Mass* (1522), *LW* 36:137-38.

[36]A difference in the concept of grace underlies much of Luther's protest against the prevailing priesthood as well as his arguments for the priesthood of all believers. Cyril Eastwood, *The Priesthood of All Believers: An Examination of the Doctrine from the Reformation to the Present Day* (Minneapolis: Augsburg, 1962), 3.

[37]Luther, *Babylonian Captivity*, *LW* 36:117.

[38]Wengert, *Priesthood*, 5.

[39]Luther, *To the Christian Nobility*, *LW* 44:126-27. Cf. *Concerning the Ministry* (1523), where Luther lodges a similar complaint: "For by a petty invention . . . the papal theory perpetuates its ministry through an *indelible character* and safeguards it against removal by any kind of wrongdoing" (*LW* 40:10). Moreover, these "walls" can be seen as a carryover from the time of the Gregorian reforms, in which clergy were protected from temporal punishment. Luther makes reference to this law in *Against the Spiritual Estate of the Pope* and argues that no leader is above reproof (*LW* 39:249-54).

[40]Luther, *Babylonian Captivity*, *LW* 36:117 (emphasis added).

[41]Speaking of the pope, Luther writes, "He divides the priestly people of Christ into clergy and laity. The clergy he calls his religious ones. . . . He makes them religious simply by tonsuring them, anointing their fingers with oil, and having them wear long garments. He claims that he is imprinting on their souls an indelible character. . . . This institution they call holy orders or ordination, one of the seven sacraments, [is made] much holier and better than baptism itself." *Misuse of the Mass*, *LW* 36:201. Cf. *Treatise on the New Testament, That Is, the Holy Mass* (1520), *LW* 35:80; *LW* 31:356.

[42]See, e.g., *Against the Spiritual Estate*, *LW* 39:268.

[43]Luther, *The Private Mass and the Consecration of Priests* (1533), *LW* 38:186-87.

[44]Luther discusses at length the proper use of the term *priest* and its synonyms in *Answer to the Hyperchristian, Hyperspiritual, and Hyperlearned*

Book by Goat Emser in Leipzig—Including Some Thoughts Regarding His Companion, the Fool Murner (1521), *LW* 39:154-55. Cf. *LW* 40:35.

[45]On the issue of celibacy and priesthood, see, e.g., *Babylonian Captivity*, *LW* 36:114, and *The Estate of Marriage* (1522), *LW* 45:46.

[46]Luther argues, "Thus [the pope] removes and eradicates our Christian priesthood with this damnable priesthood, for hardly anyone knows of any other priesthood except that of the pope. As soon as anyone hears a priest mentioned he imagines one who is tonsured, anointed and dressed in long garments." *Misuse of the Mass, LW* 36:202.

[47]Luther, *To the Christian Nobility, LW* 44:129.

[48]Luther, *Concerning the Ministry, LW* 40:20. For Luther, the priesthood of all believers is the foundation of the office of ordained priesthood.

[49]Luther, *Commentary on Psalm 110:4* (1535), *LW* 13:329.

[50]Luther, *Commentary on Psalm 110:4, LW* 13:312. Cf. *Lectures on Genesis Chapters 6–14* (1536), *LW* 2:393-94.

[51]Luther, *Misuse of the Mass, LW* 36:138.

[52]See, e.g., *LW* 13:315-24; *LW* 35:99; *LW* 36:138-39.

[53]Luther, *Misuse of the Mass, LW* 36:138.

[54]Luther, *Commentary on Psalm 110:4, LW* 13:329.

[55]Ibid., *LW* 13:330-31. "We lay ourselves on Christ by a firm faith in his testament and do not otherwise appear before God with our prayer, praise, and sacrifice except through Christ and his mediation." *Treatise on the New Testament, LW* 35:99.

[56]Luther, *Answer to the Hyperchristian, LW* 39:140-224, and *Dr. Luther's Retraction, LW* 39:229-38.

[57]Luther, *Answer to the Hyperchristian, LW* 39:151-52.

[58]Luther, *Misuse of the Mass, LW* 36:141.

[59]Luther, *Dr. Luther's Retraction, LW* 39:236.

[60]Ibid., *LW* 39:236-37.

[61]Luther, *Misuse of the Mass, LW* 36:140.

[62]Luther, *Freedom of the Christian, LW* 31:355.

[63]It should be noted that Luther does discuss believers' priesthood in his sermons, lectures and commentaries on other relevant biblical texts. See, e.g., *Lectures on Deuteronomy* (1523–1524), *LW* 9:124; *Commentary on Joel* (1524), *LW* 18:106, 109; *Commentary on Zechariah* (1527), *LW* 20:346; *Lectures on Isaiah 40–66* (1527–1530), *LW* 17:97-98, 337, 414-15; *Sermons*

on the Gospel of John 14–16 (1537), *LW* 24:242-44; and *Commentary on Psalm 51* (1538), *LW* 12:402-3.

[64]Luther, *Commentary on Psalm 110:4*, *LW* 13:315.

[65]Luther, *Misuse of the Mass*, *LW* 36:139. Here he puts access to God in place of sacrifice as part of this triad of priestly duties.

[66]Luther, *Concerning the Ministry*, *LW* 40:21. These priestly functions are highlighted in other writings as well: preaching or teaching the Word of God (*LW* 36:148-49, 152; 41:148-51; 52:139); baptism (*LW* 39:14; 41:151–44:128); celebrating the Lord's Supper (*LW* 36:116; 39:14; 41:152); binding and loosing sins (*LW* 35:12-13, 16; 39:86; 41:153); prayer (*LW* 36:139; 41:164); sacrifice (*LW* 35:99, 248; 39:235; 41:164-65); judging doctrine (*LW* 36:150; 39:305-14; 44:135).

[67]Luther, *Concerning the Ministry*, *LW* 40:21. Cf. *LW* 36:115-16.

[68]Luther, *Commentary on Psalm 110:4*, *LW* 13:333. Cf. *LW* 20:346.

[69]Luther, *Sermons on Ps 82* (1530), *LW* 13:65. Cf. *LW* 39:157; *That a Christian Assembly or Congregation Has the Right and Power to Judge All Teaching and to Call, Appoint, and Dismiss Teachers, Established and Proven by Scripture* (1523), *LW* 39:310-11. Some even took the priesthood of believers so far as to exclude the need for training for the ministry. Luther rejects this notion (see *To the Councilmen of All Cities in Germany That They Establish and Maintain Christian Schools* [1524], *LW* 45:343). Luther did make an exception to this rule. If there were no official ministers then anyone, including a woman, might preach to the congregation. The most important thing was the proclamation of the Word (*LW* 39:310; cf. *LW* 36:152).

[70]Brian A. Gerrish, "Priesthood and Ministry in the Theology of Luther," *Church History* 34 (1965): 416-17. Cf. *LW* 40:34.

[71]See *The Estate of Marriage*, *LW* 45:46; *LW* 13:333.

[72]Luther argues that any Christian could publicly preach, baptize and administer the Lord's Supper in an emergency situation, but these practices should normally be carried out by those ordained by the congregation.

[73]Luther, *Concerning the Ministry*, *LW* 40:23.

[74]Ibid., *LW* 40:24.

[75]Ibid., *LW* 40:25.

[76]Here Luther embarks on an argument against the false distinction between power and use. His opponents held that it might be true that all believers have the power of the keys, but they asserted that the use was

not common to all. Luther objects that Scripture does not make such a distinction and if it were to be upheld it would have to apply to Peter as well (Mt 16:19). Ibid., *LW* 40:26-27.

[77]The papist priests, on the other hand, bound and loosed on the basis of their own laws. In this way they undermined the gospel and closed the door of heaven to the church. Ibid., *LW* 40:28.

[78]Luther, *The Sacrament of Penance* (1519), *LW* 35:13.

[79]Luther, *Freedom of the Christian*, *LW* 31:355.

[80]Luther, *Concerning the Ministry*, *LW* 40:30.

[81]Ibid., *LW* 40:29.

[82]Luther, *Prefaces to the Old Testament* (1545), *LW* 35:248.

[83]Vilmos Vajta, *Luther on Worship: An Interpretation* (Eugene, OR: Wipf & Stock, 2004), 168-69.

[84]Luther, *Concerning the Ministry*, *LW* 40:32-33; *LW* 39:306-8; *LW* 44:135.

[85]*LW* 40:32-33.

[86]Luther, *To the Christian Nobility*, *LW* 44:136.

[87]Paul Althaus, *The Theology of Martin Luther*, trans. Robert C. Schultz (Philadelphia: Fortress, 1970), 314.

[88]Gounelle, "Le sacerdoce universel," 434.

[89]Eastwood remarks that Luther rightfully places the task of ministry *in* the church and not *above* it. He adds that the proclamation of the gospel, which is the primary ministry of the church, does not occur "outside the congregation but within it, and in this way the Gospel is mediated through the congregation." Eastwood, *Priesthood of all Believers*, 3-4.

[90]Lamin O. Sanneh, *Translating the Message: The Missionary Impact on Culture* (Maryknoll, NY: Orbis, 2009).

[91]Luther, *Prefaces to the Old Testament*, *LW* 35:247.

CHAPTER 4: LIFE IN COMMUNION

[1]The term *Christocentric-Trinitarian* comes from Michael Goheen's nuanced description of Lesslie Newbigin's ecclesiology. It was developed in dialogue with the World Council of Churches alternative proposed by Hoekendijk and Raiser—namely, "cosmoscentric-Trinitarian" ecclesiology. Michael W. Goheen, *"As the Father Has Sent Me, I Am Sending You": J. E. Lesslie Newbigin's Missionary Ecclesiology* (Zoetermeer: Boekencentrum, 2000), 64n1, 160.

[2]Cyril Eastwood, *The Royal Priesthood of the Faithful: An Investigation of the Doctrine from Biblical Times to the Reformation* (Eugene, OR: Wipf & Stock, 2009), 109-20; cf. Roman Loimeier, "Is There Something Like 'Protestant Islam'?," *Die Welt des Islams* 45, no. 2 (2005): 216-54.

[3]Joseph Fielding Smith, *Doctrines of Salvation: Sermons and Writings of Joseph Fielding Smith*, ed. Bruce R. McConkie (Salt Lake City, UT: Bookcraft, 1954), 3:132. Cf. Douglas James Davies, *An Introduction to Mormonism* (New York: Cambridge University Press, 2003), 175.

[4]Martin Luther, *Commentary on Psalm 110:4* (1535), *LW* 13:323.

[5]Fred Sanders, *The Deep Things of God: How the Trinity Changes Everything* (Wheaton, IL: Crossway, 2010), 168 (emphasis added).

[6]Of course Luther did not completely ignore the Spirit; see his discussion of Psalm 110:3 and 1 Peter 4:10 (*LW* 13:294-95; 30:123-24). See further Howard A. Snyder, *The Community of the King* (Downers Grove, IL: InterVarsity Press, 2004), 113; Paul R. Hinlicky, *Paths Not Taken: Fates of Theology from Luther Through Leibniz* (Grand Rapids: Eerdmans, 2009), 127-28, 170-76.

[7]See further Ingemar Öberg, *Luther and World Mission: A Historical and Systematic Study with Special Reference to Luther's Bible Exposition*, trans. Dean Apel (St. Louis: Concordia, 2007), 501.

[8]Lesslie Newbigin, *The Open Secret: An Introduction to the Theology of Mission* (Grand Rapids: Eerdmans, 1995), 61 (emphasis added).

[9]Lesslie Newbigin, *Unfinished Agenda: An Updated Autobiography* (Grand Rapids: Eerdmans, 1993), 144.

[10]Lesslie Newbigin, "Ministry and Laity," *National Christian Council Review* 85 (1965): 480.

[11]Lesslie Newbigin, *The Gospel in a Pluralistic Society* (Grand Rapids: Eerdmans, 1989), 229 (emphasis added).

[12]"Again, each individual is responsible for its actually being a missionary community. . . . We have to remember that every Christian is to be a missionary, a recruiting officer for new witnesses. If our congregations do not recognize this and act accordingly, they cannot be missionary congregations, and therefore they cannot be truly Christian." Karl Barth, *Church Dogmatics* III/4, trans. G. W. Bromiley and T. F. Torrance (Edinburgh: T&T Clark, 1961), 505.

[13]"Our first task, therefore, must be to consider how to teach trinitarian religion, how to initiate our congregations into the trinitarian way of life.

. . . It is better that we should enrich our spiritual life by exploring to the full the possibilities of our threefold relationship to Him than that for fear of Tritheism we should impoverish it and never enter fully into the heritage of our Christian revelation." Leonard Hodgson, *The Doctrine of the Trinity*, Croall Lectures, 1942–1943 (London: Nisbet, 1943), 177, 180.

[14]Ibid., 179 (emphasis added).

[15]John Owen, *Communion with the Triune God*, ed. Kelly M. Kapic and Justin Taylor (Wheaton, IL: Crossway, 2007), 95, 101. See also J. I. Packer, "A Puritan Perspective: Trinitarian Godliness According to John Owen," in *God the Holy Trinity: Reflections on Christian Faith and Practice*, ed. Timothy George (Grand Rapids: Baker Academic, 2006), 91-108.

[16]See further Sanders, *Deep Things of God*, for helpful discussions of "tacit trinitarianism" and how evangelicals experience the Trinity through prayer and Bible reading.

[17]Friedrich Schleiermacher, *The Christian Faith*, ed. Hugh Ross Mackintosh and J. S. Stewart (New York: T&T Clark, 1928), 741; Immanuel Kant, *Religion and Rational Theology*, ed. Allen W. Wood and George Di Giovanni (New York: Cambridge University Press, 1996), 264.

[18]"Father, Son, and Spirit are irreducibly distinct personal agents in their interaction not only with one another, but with us. The divine actions of creation and salvation therefore establish a relationship with creatures unique to each of the divine persons." Bruce Marshall is here stating a general consensus. "Trinity," in *The Blackwell Companion to Modern Theology*, ed. Gareth Jones (Malden, MA: Blackwell, 2004), 188. Cf. Gilles Emery, *The Trinity: An Introduction to Catholic Doctrine on the Triune God*, trans. Matthew Levering (Washington, DC: Catholic University of America Press, 2011), 164-65.

[19]Karl Barth, *Church Dogmatics* I/1 (Edinburgh: T&T Clark, 1956), 375, 395.

[20]The description of *perichoresis* as a divine dance has been misused of late, but it remains a helpful analogy for those encountering the doctrine for the first time. See Edith Humphrey, *Grand Entrance: Worship on Earth as in Heaven* (Grand Rapids: Brazos, 2011), 70.

[21]Kathryn Tanner, "The Trinity," in *The Blackwell Companion to Political Theology*, ed. Peter Scott and William T. Cavanaugh, Blackwell Companions to Religion (Oxford: Blackwell, 2006), 328-31.

[22]Augustine, *The Trinity* I.4, trans. Stephen McKenna, FC 45 (New York: Fathers of the Church, 1962), 11; Barth, *CD* I/1, 375; Keith E. Johnson,

"Augustine's 'Trinitarian' Reading of John 5: A Model for the Theological Interpretation of Scripture?," *Journal of the Evangelical Theological Society* 52, no. 4 (2009): 808-10; Henri Blocher, "Immanence and Transcendence in Trinitarian Theology," in *The Trinity in a Pluralistic Age: Theological Essays on Culture and Religion*, ed. Kevin Vanhoozer (Grand Rapids: Eerdmans, 1997), 120.

[23]By *properties* I refer especially to paternity, filiation and procession. This definition is adapted from Emery, *The Trinity*, 165-66; Barth, *CD* I/1, 373-74; and Thomas Aquinas, *Summa Theologica* 1.39.7.

[24]Compare John Calvin's comments in *Institutes of the Christian Religion* 1.13.18, ed. John Thomas McNeill, trans. Ford Lewis Battles, Library of Christian Classics 21 (Philadelphia: Westminster, 1960), 142-43.

[25]Augustine, *Trinity* 1.3.5 (FC 45:8) (emphasis added).

[26]Basil the Great, *On the Holy Spirit* 16.35, trans. David Anderson (Crestwood, NY: St. Vladimir's Seminary Press, 1980), 70.

[27]See discussion in Roger E. Olson and Christopher A. Hall, *The Trinity*, Guides to Theology (Grand Rapids: Eerdmans, 2002), 58.

[28]Athanasius, *Letters to Serapion* 1.28.3 (PP 43:97).

[29]See the helpful discussion of this analogy in Sanders, *Deep Things of God*, 212-14.

[30]Blocher, "Immanence and Transcendence in Trinitarian Theology," 122.

[31]Barth, *CD* I/1, 397.

[32]"Dad" is a better contemporary English translation of *Abba* than "Father" or "Daddy."

[33]Luke 10:21; John 11:41; 12:27-28; 17:1-26; Matthew 26:39, 42 // Mark 14:36 // Luke 22:42; Luke 23:34; Matthew 27:46 = Ps 22:1 (Jesus' only prayer without explicit reference to his Father); and Luke 23:46.

[34]See also John 4:20-24; Hebrews 13:15.

[35]1 Peter 1:2, 3, 21; 2:4; 3:18, 22; 4:11; 5:10.

[36]Barth, *CD* I/1, 395.

[37]See David Kupp, *Matthew's Emmanuel: Divine Presence and God's People in the First Gospel* (New York: Cambridge University Press, 1996), 196-98, 230-33.

[38]There are at least nine Hebrew and Greek words or phrases behind the English concept of "world." For a discussion of these words and their relation to the English concept, see Christopher J. H. Wright, "The World in the Bible," *Evangelical Review of Theology* 34 (2010): 208-9.

[39]Yves Congar, *Lay People in the Church: A Study for a Theology of Laity*, trans. Donald Attwater, rev. ed. (Westminster, MD: Newman, 1967). For an important Orthodox study that comes to many of the same conclusions, see Nicholas Afanasiev, *The Church of the Holy Spirit*, ed. Michael Plekon, trans. Vitaly Permiakov (Notre Dame, IN: University of Notre Dame Press, 2007).

[40]Yves M. J. Congar, "My Path-Findings in the Theology of Laity and Ministries," *The Jurist* 32 (1972): 176.

[41]Michael Scott Horton, *The Christian Faith: A Systematic Theology for Pilgrims on the Way* (Grand Rapids: Zondervan, 2011), 897. Elsewhere Horton identifies the "church" as synonymous with the "clergy," an error not uncommon among the magisterial reformers. "We even refuse the label 'ministry,' reserving that hallowed noun for the church." Horton, "The Church After the Parachurch," *Modern Reformation* 21 (2012): 53.

[42]George Barna, *Revolution: Finding Vibrant Faith Beyond the Walls of the Sanctuary* (Wheaton, IL: Tyndale, 2005), 8, 131.

[43]Ibid., 3. The 2012 edition begins differently, but its narrative remains problematic.

[44]Reinhold Niebuhr, *The Nature and Destiny of Man: A Christian Interpretation* (London: Nisbet, 1949), 201.

[45]For background on this issue, see Nijay Gupta, "Which 'Body' Is a Temple (1 Corinthians 6:19)? Paul Beyond the Individual/Communal Divide," *Catholic Biblical Quarterly* 72 (2010): 518-36.

[46]Newbigin, *The Open Secret*, 32.

[47]One of the best books to be written on the priesthood of all believers in the last twenty years, Peter Leithart's *The Priesthood of the Plebs*, needs critique on this point.

[48]Newbigin, *The Open Secret*, 56.

Chapter 5: Worship, Work and Witness

[1]See also Revelation 3:21 and 7:15.

[2]N. T. Wright, *After You Believe: Why Christian Character Matters* (New York: HarperCollins, 2010), 67.

[3]Miroslav Volf, "Theology for a Way of Life," in *Practicing Theology: Beliefs and Practices in Christian Life*, ed. Miroslav Volf and Dorothy C. Bass (Grand Rapids: Eerdmans, 2002), 247 (emphasis original).

[4]Thomas F. Torrance, *Christian Doctrine of God, One Being Three Persons* (New York: T&T Clark, 2001), 134.

[5]Dallas Willard, *Renovation of the Heart: Putting on the Character of Christ* (Colorado Springs, CO: NavPress, 2002), 77-94.

[6]Jonathan R. Wilson, *Why Church Matters: Worship, Ministry, and Mission in Practice* (Grand Rapids: Brazos, 2006), 20. See further L. Roger Owens, *The Shape of Participation: A Theology of Church Practices* (Eugene, OR: Cascade, 2010).

[7]See discussion of Irenaeus's view of the baptismal anointing in Kilian McDonnell, *The Baptism of Jesus in the Jordan: The Trinitarian and Cosmic Order of Salvation* (Collegeville, MN: Liturgical, 1996), 116-23.

[8]W. A. M. Beuken, "The Main Theme of Trito-Isaiah, 'The Servants of Yhwh,'" *Journal for the Study of the Old Testament* 47 (1990): 67-87.

[9]See discussion of Tertullian's "oath of baptism" in Peter Cramer, *Baptism and Change in the Early Middle Ages, C. 200-C. 1150* (New York: Cambridge University Press, 1993), 63. Those communions committed to paedobaptism usually have sponsors who "speak on behalf of the infants and younger children"; *The Book of Common Prayer* (New York: Seabury, 1977), 302.

[10]There are other proposals. Nancey Murphy, in conversation with John Yoder, argues for discernment, discipling (including "binding and loosing"), worship, works of mercy and witness as "the practices constitutive of the church's mission and identity." Nancey C. Murphy, Brad J. Kallenberg and Mark Nation, eds., *Virtues & Practices in the Christian Tradition: Christian Ethics After MacIntyre* (Harrisburg, PA: Trinity, 1997), 37, see also 132. Robert Muthiah focuses on five practices (witness; Lord's Supper, discernment, friendship and confession), with significant overlap to the seven proposed in this chapter. *The Priesthood of All Believers in the Twenty-First Century: Living Faithfully as the Whole People of God in a Postmodern Context* (Eugene, OR: Wipf & Stock, 2009), 134-73. Others focus on the importance of "creational practices" such as hospitality, marriage, parenting and celibacy.

[11]Martin Luther, *Concerning the Ministry*, LW 40:21-34. This is the only place where Luther treats all seven of these practices in a single location, although he treats them individually or in smaller groups in numerous places. Significantly, his list of seven essential practices changes by 1539 (*On the Councils and the Church*, LW 41:143-78; WA 50:509-653).

[12]Karl Barth, *The Christian Life, Church Dogmatics IV/4: Lecture Fragments*, trans. Geoffrey W. Bromiley (Grand Rapids: Eerdmans, 1981), 45-46.

[13]Many will recognize that this definition is adapted from Alasdair MacIntyre, *After Virtue: A Study in Moral Theory*, 2nd ed. (Notre Dame, IN: University of Notre Dame Press, 1984), 187. See further Jonathan R. Wilson, *Living Faithfully in a Fragmented World: Lessons for the Church from MacIntyre's After Virtue* (Harrisburg, PA: Trinity, 1997).

[14]Don Davis, *Sacred Roots: A Primer on Retrieving the Great Tradition* (Wichita, KS: The Urban Ministry Institute, 2010), 49-58.

[15]For Augustine, every thought, word or deed that was aimed at God could be considered a spiritual sacrifice. See *City of God* 10.6 (FC 14:125); *The Trinity* 4.14 (FC 45:155).

[16]Raymond Corriveau, *The Liturgy of Life: A Study of the Ethical Thought of St. Paul in His Letters to the Early Christian Communities* (Montreal: Desclée De Brouwer, 1970).

[17]The latter portion of the rule is usually stated as *servato discrimine et ordine personarum*. See further Henri Blocher, "Immanence and Transcendence in Trinitarian Theology," in *The Trinity in a Pluralistic Age: Theological Essays on Culture and Religion*, ed. Kevin Vanhoozer (Grand Rapids: Eerdmans, 1997), 120.

[18]It is also one of the few "once-for-all" washings in the Old Testament. See also Exodus 40:12 and Leviticus 8:6. On John's baptism and Levitical baptisms see Leithart, *Priesthood of the Plebs*, 95.

[19]Tertullian, *On Baptism* 7 (ANF 3:672).

[20]Susan K. Wood, *One Baptism: Ecumenical Dimensions of the Doctrine of Baptism* (Collegeville, MN: Liturgical, 2009), 12. Paul Dabin traces the theme of the royal priesthood's commissioning at baptism through the thought of some 350 theologians in his *Le Sacerdoce Royal Des Fidèles Dans la Tradicion Ancienne et Moderne* (Paris: L'Edition Universelle, 1950).

[21]Thomas Torrance, *Royal Priesthood: A Theology of Ordained Ministry*, 2nd ed. (New York: T&T Clark, 1993), 34.

[22]Karl Barth, *CD* IV/4, 50-68.

[23]Martin Luther, *WA* 51:111. English translation in Jaroslav Pelikan, "Once for All the Sacrifice of Himself (Heb 9:26)," in *Luther the Expositor* (St. Louis: Concordia, 1959), 251.

[24]See chapter 2 note 55 above.

[25]Tertullian, *On Idolatry* 19 (ANF 3:73).

[26]See discussion in Tertullian, *On Baptism* 7 (ANF 3:672).

[27]See discussion in Irenaeus, *Against Heresies* 3.17.1 (ANF 1:444).

[28]Even those who see the "baptism of the Holy Spirit" as "distinct from and additional to His regenerating work" emphasize that the empowering of the Holy Spirit "is always connected with and primarily for the purpose of testimony and service." R. A. Torrey, *The Person and Work of the Holy Spirit* (Grand Rapids: Zondervan, 1974), 149, 153.

[29]See the discussion of twenty-one types of prayer in Richard Foster, *Prayer: Finding the Heart's True Home* (Grand Rapids: Zondervan, 2002).

[30]Romans 8:34 and Hebrews 7:25 (cf. Heb 9:24) describe Christ's role as priestly intercessor, with reference to Psalm 110:1-4.

[31]Graham Redding, *Prayer and the Priesthood of Christ: In the Reformed Tradition* (New York: T&T Clark, 2003), 286.

[32]Dietrich Bonhoeffer, *Life Together* (New York: Harper & Row, 1954), 86-87.

[33]For a good introduction to the Lord's Prayer, see John Calvin, *Institutes* III.20 (Library of Christian Classics 21:850-920).

[34]Jesus called God his "Father" more than 160 times in the Gospels. As the Father "in heaven" he is different from earthly fathers. He is a heavenly Father with a "motherly touch." See further John W. Cooper, *Our Father in Heaven: Christian Faith and Inclusive Language for God* (Grand Rapids: Baker, 1998).

[35]Dietrich Bonhoeffer, *Psalms: The Prayer Book of the Bible* (Minneapolis: Fortress, 1974), 16.

[36]Ibid., 11.

[37]The pastor has also written an excellent book on the Psalms. See Patrick Henry Reardon, *Christ in the Psalms* (Ben Lomond, CA: Conciliar Press, 2000).

[38]Lamin O. Sanneh, *Translating the Message: The Missionary Impact on Culture* (Maryknoll, NY: Orbis, 2009).

[39]Martin Luther, *Preface to the First Five Books of Moses*, LW 35:248.

[40]Augustine, *On Christian Teaching* 2.16, 19.

[41]C. S. Lewis, *Reflections on the Psalms* (Glasgow: Collins, 1978), 79, 81.

[42]R. W. L. Moberly, *The Bible, Theology, and Faith: A Study of Abraham and Jesus* (New York: Cambridge University Press, 2000), 182.

[43]Dietrich Bonhoeffer, "Instructions in Daily Meditation," in *Meditating on the Word*, trans. David McI. Gracie (Cambridge, MA: Cowley, 1986), 21-27.

[44]Hank Voss, "From 'Grammatical-Historical Exegesis' to 'Theological Exegesis': Five Essential Practices," *Evangelical Review of Theology* 37 (2013): 140-52.

[45]Thomas C. Oden, *Corrective Love: The Power of Communion Discipline* (St. Louis: Concordia, 1995), 56.

[46]On the tabernacle, see Leviticus 10:1-10; Numbers 3:5-10; 18:1-7; on sabbath and holy days, see Exodus 34:18; Leviticus 26:2; Deuteronomy 5:12-15; on guarding covenant, see Exodus 19:5; 32:26-29.

[47]Richard Hays, *The Moral Vision of the New Testament: Community, Cross, New Creation; A Contemporary Introduction to New Testament Ethics* (San Francisco: HarperCollins, 1996), 101-4.

[48]Martin Luther, *The Babylonian Captivity of the Church*, LW 36:81-90, cf. 124; and Jaroslav Pelikan, *Spirit Versus Structure: Luther and the Institutions of the Church* (New York: Harper & Row, 1968), 28-30, 126-30.

[49]Luther, *The Sacrament of Penance* (1519), LW 35:16, cf. 12.

[50]Balthasar Hubmaier, *Balthasar Hubmaier, Theologian of Anabaptism*, ed. John Howard Yoder and H. Wayne Pipkin (Scottdale, PA: Herald, 1989), 387.

[51]For more on confrontation, confession, forgiveness and restoration, see L. Gregory Jones, *Embodying Forgiveness: A Theological Analysis* (Grand Rapids: Eerdmans, 1995); Oden, *Corrective Love*, 205-11; John R. W. Stott, *Confess Your Sins: The Way of Reconciliation* (Waco, TX: Word, 1965); Desmond Tutu, *No Future Without Forgiveness* (New York: Doubleday, 2000).

[52]Bonhoeffer, *Life Together*, 111-12.

[53]Leithart, *Priesthood of the Plebs*, 64-71.

[54]T. F. Torrance, "Service in Jesus Christ," in *Service in Christ: Essays Presented to Karl Barth on His 80th Birthday*, ed. James I. McCord and T. H. L. Parker (Grand Rapids: Eerdmans, 1966), 1.

[55]John Howard Yoder, *The Fullness of Christ: Paul's Revolutionary Vision of Universal Ministry* (Elgin, IL: Brethren, 1987).

[56]For this translation, see discussion in James Ware, *The Mission of the Church in Paul's Letter to the Philippians in the Context of Ancient Judaism* (Boston: Brill, 2005), 256-84.

[57]This was Lesslie Newbigin's preferred way of speaking about the church. Goheen, *Lesslie Newbigin's Missionary Ecclesiology*, 172.

[58]See discussion in Nicholas Perrin, *Jesus the Temple* (Grand Rapids: Baker Academic, 2010), 114-48.

[59]For example, Alberto Roldán, "The Priesthood of All Believers and Integral Mission," in *The Local Church, Agent of Transformation: An Ecclesiology for Integral Mission*, ed. Tetsunao Yamamori and C. René Padilla, trans. Brian Cordingly (Buenos Aires: Kairós, 2004).

[60]Many of these activities are discussed in Paul W. Chilcote and Laceye C. Warner, eds., *The Study of Evangelism: Exploring a Missional Practice of the Church* (Grand Rapids: Eerdmans, 2008).

[61]Outside the New Testament, the earliest Christian writings usually refer to the Lord's Supper as the Eucharist ("thanksgiving"). See *Didache* 9–10; Justin Martyr, *1 Apology* 65; Ignatius, *Epistle to Smyrnaeans* 6:2; as well as the discussion in Andrew B. McGowan, *Ancient Christian Worship: Early Church Practices in Social, Historical, and Theological Perspective* (Grand Rapids: Baker Academic, 2014), 19-64.

[62]Thomas Aquinas, *Summa Theologica* 3.65.3.

[63]Everett Ferguson, *The Church of Christ: A Biblical Ecclesiology for Today* (Grand Rapids: Eerdmans, 1996), 249 (emphasis added).

[64]Each word is treated in its own chapter. Gordon T. Smith, *A Holy Meal: The Lord's Supper in the Life of the Church* (Grand Rapids: Baker Academic, 2005).

[65]The forgiveness Jesus displayed when he ate with sinners was shocking to many of the religious people of Jesus' day. His radical forgiveness remains at the core of faithful celebrations of the Lord's Supper today. See Geoffrey Wainwright, *Eucharist and Eschatology*, 3rd ed. (Peterborough: Epworth, 2002), 33-34.

[66]Theologians in the Puritan tradition, such as Jonathan Edwards, emphasized the renewal of our baptismal covenants each time we come to the Lord's Supper. See discussion in Smith, *Holy Meal*, 67-79.

CHAPTER 6: REPRESENTING CHRIST

[1]Don Davis, *Sacred Roots: A Primer on Retrieving the Great Tradition* (Wichita, KS: The Urban Ministry Institute, 2010), 41-45.

[2]James Ware, *The Mission of the Church in Paul's Letter to the Philippians*

in the Context of Ancient Judaism (Boston: Brill, 2005), 272-73.

[3]Kevin Vanhoozer, *The Drama of Doctrine: A Canonical-Linguistic Approach to Christian Theology* (Louisville, KY: Westminster John Knox, 2005).

[4]Isaiah 56–66 actually has a chiastic structure, with Isaiah 61 at the emphatic center. Details of the chiasm vary; for discussion, see Gary Smith, *Isaiah 40–66* (Nashville, TN: B&H Academic, 2009), 520-22.

[5]Translation modified from Michael Lattke, *Odes of Solomon: A Commentary*, trans. Marianne Erhardt (Minneapolis: Fortress, 2009), 285; cf. James Charlesworth, ed., "Odes of Solomon," in *The Old Testament Pseudepigrapha*, vol. 2 (Garden City, NY: Doubleday, 1985), 753.

BIBLIOGRAPHY

Achtemeier, Paul J. *1 Peter: A Commentary on First Peter*. Hermeneia. Minneapolis: Fortress, 1996.

Afanasiev, Nicholas. *The Church of the Holy Spirit*. Edited by Michael Plekon. Translated by Vitaly Permiakov. Notre Dame, IN: University of Notre Dame Press, 2007.

Allen, Leslie C. *Psalms 101–150*. Word Biblical Commentary 21. Waco, TX: Word, 1983.

Althaus, Paul. *The Theology of Martin Luther*. Translated by Robert C. Schultz. Philadelphia: Fortress, 1970.

Athanasius. *Works on the Spirit: Athanasius's Letters to Serapion on the Holy Spirit, and, Didymus's on the Holy Spirit*. Translated by Mark DelCogliano, Andrew Radde-Gallwitz and Lewis Ayres. Yonkers, NY: St. Vladimir's Seminary Press, 2011.

Augustine. *De Doctrina Christiana*. Translated by R. P. H. Green. OECT. New York: Clarendon, 1995.

———. *The Trinity*. Translated by Stephen McKenna. Fathers of the Church 45. New York: Fathers of the Church, 1962.

Austen, Jane. *Pride and Prejudice*. Edited by Joseph Pearce. San Francisco: Ignatius, 2008.

Barker, Margaret. *The Gate of Heaven: The History and Symbolism of the Temple in Jerusalem*. London: SPCK, 1991.

Barna, George. *Revolution: Finding Vibrant Faith Beyond the Walls of the Sanctuary*. Wheaton, IL: Tyndale House, 2005.

Barth, Karl. *The Christian Life: Church Dogmatics IV, 4: Lecture Fragments.* Translated by Geoffrey W. Bromiley. Grand Rapids: Eerdmans, 1981.

———. *Church Dogmatics* I/1. Edinburgh: T&T Clark, 1956.

Basil the Great. *On the Holy Spirit.* Translated by David Anderson. Crestwood, NY: St. Vladimir's Seminary Press, 1980.

Beale, G. K. *The Book of Revelation.* New International Greek Testament Commentary. Grand Rapids: Eerdmans, 1999.

———. *The Temple and the Church's Mission: A Biblical Theology of the Dwelling Place of God.* New Studies in Biblical Theology 17. Downers Grove, IL: IVP Academic, 2003.

Beale, G. K., and Mitchell Kim. *God Dwells Among Us: Expanding Eden to the Ends of the Earth.* Downers Grove, IL: InterVarsity Press, 2014.

Beasley-Murray, Paul. "Romans 1:3f: An Early Confession of Faith in the Lordship of Jesus." *Tyndale Bulletin* 31 (1980): 147-54.

Bénétreau, Samuel. *La Premiere Epitre de Pierre.* Commentaire Evangelique de la Bible. Vaux-sur-Seine: Edifac, 1992.

———. *L'Epitre aux Hebreux.* 2 vols. Commentaire Evangelique de la Bible. Paris: Edifac, 1989–1990.

Best, Ernest. "Spiritual Sacrifice: General Priesthood in the New Testament." *Interpretation* 14 (1960): 273-99.

Beuken, W. A. M. "The Main Theme of Trito-Isaiah, 'The Servants of Yhwh.'" *Journal for the Study of the Old Testament* 47 (1990): 67-87.

Blocher, Henri. "Immanence and Transcendence in Trinitarian Theology." In *The Trinity in a Pluralistic Age: Theological Essays on Culture and Religion,* edited by Kevin Vanhoozer, 104-23. Grand Rapids: Eerdmans, 1997.

Blumenthal, Uta-Renate. *The Investiture Controversy: Church and Monarchy from the Ninth to the Twelfth Century.* Philadelphia: University of Pennsylvania Press, 1988.

Bonhoeffer, Dietrich. "Instructions in Daily Meditation." In *Meditating on the Word,* translated by David McI. Gracie, 21-27. Cambridge, MA: Cowley, 1986.

———. *Life Together.* New York: Harper & Row, 1954.

———. *Life Together; Prayerbook of the Bible*. Edited by Geffrey Kelly. Translated by Daniel Bloesch and James Burtness. Minneapolis: Fortress, 2006.

———. *Psalms: The Prayer Book of the Bible*. Minneapolis: Fortress, 1974.

Bradshaw, Paul F. *Ordination Rites of the Ancient Churches of East and West*. New York: Pueblo, 1990.

Brock, Sebastian. "The Priesthood of the Baptised: Some Syriac Perspectives." *Sobornost* 9 (1987): 14-22.

Brueggemann, Walter. *Genesis*. Interpretation: A Bible Commentary for Teaching and Preaching. Atlanta: John Knox, 1982.

Bulley, Colin. *The Priesthood of Some Believers: Developments from the General to the Special Priesthood in the Christian Literature of the First Three Centuries*. Paternoster Biblical and Theological Monographs. Waynesboro, GA: Paternoster, 2000.

Calvin, Jean. *Institutes of the Christian Religion*. Edited by John Thomas McNeill. Translated by Ford Lewis Battles. 2 vols. Library of Christian Classics. Philadelphia: Westminster, 1960.

Carroll Rodas, M. Daniel. "La Misión Integral: Ser Bendición: Un Aporte Desde El Antiguo Testamento." *Kairós* 36 (2005): 25-38.

Catechism of the Catholic Church. New York: Doubleday, 1995.

Charlesworth, James, ed. "Odes of Solomon." In *The Old Testament Pseudepigrapha*, 2:725-71. Garden City, NY: Doubleday, 1985.

Chilcote, Paul W., and Laceye C. Warner, eds. *The Study of Evangelism: Exploring a Missional Practice of the Church*. Grand Rapids: Eerdmans, 2008.

Clines, D. J. A. "The Image of God in Man." *Tyndale Bulletin* 19 (1968): 53-103.

Congar, Yves. *Lay People in the Church: A Study for a Theology of Laity*. Translated by Donald Attwater. Rev. ed. Westminster, MD: Newman, 1967.

———. "My Path-Findings in the Theology of Laity and Ministries." *The Jurist* 32 (1972): 168-88.

Cooper, John W. *Our Father in Heaven: Christian Faith and Inclusive Language for God*. Grand Rapids: Baker, 1998.

Corriveau, Raymond. *The Liturgy of Life: A Study of the Ethical Thought of St. Paul in His Letters to the Early Christian Communities*. Montreal: Desclée De Brouwer, 1970.

Cramer, Peter. *Baptism and Change in the Early Middle Ages, C. 200–C. 1150*. New York: Cambridge University Press, 1993.

Cullman, Oscar. *The Christology of the New Testament*. Translated by Shirley C. Guthrie and Charles A. M. Hall. Philadelphia: Westminster John Knox, 1959.

Dabin, Paul. *Le Sacerdoce Royal Des Fidèles Dans La Tradicion Ancienne et Moderne*. Paris: L'Edition Universelle, 1950.

Davies, Douglas James. *An Introduction to Mormonism*. New York: Cambridge University Press, 2003.

Davies, John A. *A Royal Priesthood: Literary and Intertextual Perspectives on an Image of Israel in Exodus 19:6*. Journal for the Study of the Old Testament: Supplement Series 395. London: T&T Clark, 2004.

Davis, Don. *Evangelism and Spiritual Warfare*. Capstone Curriculum 8. Wichita, KS: The Urban Ministry Institute, 2005.

———. *Sacred Roots: A Primer on Retrieving the Great Tradition*. Wichita, KS: The Urban Ministry Institute, 2010.

Denzinger, Henry, ed. *The Sources of Catholic Dogma*. Translated by Roy J. Deferrari. St. Louis: B. Herder, 1957.

Dion, Paul E. "Ressemblance et Image de Dieu: Égypte et Mésopotamie." In *Supplément au Dictionnaire de la Bible*, edited by L. Pirot and A. Robert, 10:366-75. Paris: Letouzey & Ané, 1985.

Dumbrell, William J. *The Search for Order: Biblical Eschatology in Focus*. Grand Rapids: Baker, 1994.

Eastwood, Cyril. *The Priesthood of All Believers: An Examination of the Doctrine from the Reformation to the Present Day*. Minneapolis: Augsburg, 1962.

———. *The Royal Priesthood of the Faithful: An Investigation of the Doctrine from Biblical Times to the Reformation*. London: Epworth, 1963; repr., Eugene, OR: Wipf & Stock, 2009.

Elliott, John H. *The Elect and the Holy: An Exegetical Examination of*

1 Peter 2:4-10 and the Phrase Basileion Hierateuma. Novum Testamentum Supplements 12. Leiden: Brill, 1966.

———. *1 Peter: A New Translation with Introduction and Commentary.* Anchor Bible 37B. New York: Doubleday, 2000.

Fee, Gordon D. *Paul's Letter to the Philippians.* New International Commentary on the New Testament. Grand Rapids: Eerdmans, 1995.

Ferguson, Everett, ed. *Encyclopedia of Early Christianity.* 2nd ed. New York: Garland, 1997.

Fletcher-Louis, Crispin H. T. "Jesus as the High Priestly Messiah: Part 1." *Journal for the Study of the Historical Jesus* 4 (2006): 155-75.

———. "Jesus as the High Priestly Messiah: Part 2." *Journal for the Study of the Historical Jesus* 5 (2007): 57-79.

Floor, Lambertus. "The General Priesthood of Believers in the Epistle to the Hebrews." In *Ad Hebraeos: Essays on the Epistle to the Hebrews*, 72-82. Pretoria: Die Nuwe-Testamentiese Werkgemeenskap van Suid-Afrika, 1971.

Foster, Richard J. *Prayer: Finding the Heart's True Home.* Grand Rapids: Zondervan, 2002.

Fretheim, Terence E. "Genesis." In *The New Interpreters Bible*, vol. 1. Nashville, TN: Abingdon, 1994.

Gentry, Peter J. "Kingdom Through Covenant: Humanity as the Divine Image." *Southern Baptist Journal of Theology* 12 (2008): 16-42.

Gerrish, Brian A. "Priesthood and Ministry in the Theology of Luther." *Church History* 34 (1965): 404-22.

Goheen, Michael. *"As the Father Has Sent Me, I Am Sending You": Lesslie Newbigin's Missionary Ecclesiology.* Zoetermeer: Boekencentrum, 2000.

Gounelle, André. "Le sacerdoce universel." Études *Théologiques et Religieuses* 63 (1988): 429-34.

Gunton, Colin E. "The Community: The Trinity and the Being of the Church." In *The Promise of Trinitarian Theology*, 58-85. Edinburgh: T&T Clark, 1991.

Gupta, Nijay. "Which 'Body' Is a Temple (1 Corinthians 6:19)? Paul

Beyond the Individual/Communal Divide." *Catholic Biblical Quarterly* 72 (2010): 518-36.

Hay, David. *Glory at the Right Hand: Psalm 110 in Early Christianity.* Nashville, TN: Abingdon, 1973.

Hays, Richard. *The Moral Vision of the New Testament: Community, Cross, New Creation; A Contemporary Introduction to New Testament Ethics.* San Francisco: HarperCollins, 1996.

Hinlicky, Paul R. *Paths Not Taken: Fates of Theology from Luther Through Leibniz.* Grand Rapids: Eerdmans, 2009.

Hodgson, Leonard. *The Doctrine of the Trinity.* Croall Lectures, 1942–1943. London: Nisbet, 1943.

Horton, Michael S. *The Christian Faith: A Systematic Theology for Pilgrims on the Way.* Grand Rapids: Zondervan, 2011.

———. "The Church After the Parachurch." *Modern Reformation* 2 (2012): 50-53.

Hubmaier, Balthasar. *Balthasar Hubmaier, Theologian of Anabaptism.* Edited by John Howard Yoder and H. Wayne Pipkin. Scottdale, PA: Herald, 1989.

Hugo, Victor. *Les Misérables.* New York: Random House, 2008.

Humphrey, Edith. *Grand Entrance: Worship on Earth as in Heaven.* Grand Rapids: Brazos, 2011.

Johnson, Keith E. "Augustine's 'Trinitarian' Reading of John 5: A Model for the Theological Interpretation of Scripture?" *Journal of the Evangelical Theological Society* 52, no. 4 (2009): 799-810.

Jones, L. Gregory. *Embodying Forgiveness: A Theological Analysis.* Grand Rapids: Eerdmans, 1995.

Kant, Immanuel. *Religion and Rational Theology.* Edited by Allen W. Wood and George Di Giovanni. New York: Cambridge University Press, 1996.

Kline, Meredith G. *Images of the Spirit.* Grand Rapids: Baker, 1980.

Küng, Hans. *The Church.* Translated by Ray and Rosaleen Ockenden. New York: Sheed and Ward, 1967.

Kupp, David. *Matthew's Emmanuel: Divine Presence and God's People in the First Gospel.* New York: Cambridge University Press, 1996.

Lane, William L. *The Gospel According to Mark.* New International Commentary on the New Testament. Grand Rapids: Eerdmans, 1974.

———. *Hebrews 1–8.* Word Biblical Commentary 47A. Dallas: Word, 1991.

Lattke, Michael. *Odes of Solomon: A Commentary.* Translated by Marianne Erhardt. Minneapolis: Fortress, 2009.

Leithart, Peter. *The Priesthood of the Plebs: A Theology of Baptism.* Eugene, OR: Wipf & Stock, 2003.

Letham, Robert. *The Holy Trinity: In Scripture, History, Theology, and Worship.* Phillipsburg, NJ: P&R, 2004.

Lewis, C. S. *Reflections on the Psalms.* Glasgow: Collins, 1978.

Liechty, Daniel, ed. *Early Anabaptist Spirituality: Selected Writings.* Mahwah, NJ: Paulist, 1994.

Limburg, James. "The Responsibility of Royalty: Genesis 1–11 and the Care of the Earth." *Word and World* 11 (1991): 124-30.

Littell, Franklin H. "The Radical Reformation." In *The Layman in Christian History: A Project of the Department on the Laity of the World Council of Churches,* edited by Stephen C. Neill and Hans Ruedi Weber, 260-75. Philadelphia: Westminster, 1963.

Lohfink, Norbert. *Theology of the Pentateuch: Themes of the Priestly Narrative and Deuteronomy.* Translated by Linda M. Malone. Minneapolis: Fortress, 1994.

Loimeier, Roman. "Is There Something Like 'Protestant Islam'?" *Die Welt Des Islams* 45, no. 2 (2005): 216-54.

Lubac, Henri de. *The Splendor of the Church.* San Francisco: Ignatius, 1999.

MacIntyre, Alasdair. *After Virtue: A Study in Moral Theory.* 2nd ed. Notre Dame, IN: University of Notre Dame Press, 1984.

Marshall, Bruce D. "Trinity." In *The Blackwell Companion to Modern Theology,* edited by Gareth Jones, 183-203. Blackwell Companions to Religion. Malden, MA: Blackwell, 2004.

McConville, J. G. *Deuteronomy.* Apollos Old Testament Commentary 5. Downers Grove, IL: IVP Academic, 2002.

McDonnell, Kilian. *The Baptism of Jesus in the Jordan: The Trinitarian and Cosmic Order of Salvation*. Collegeville, MN: Liturgical, 1996.

McGowan, Andrew B. *Ancient Christian Worship: Early Church Practices in Social, Historical, and Theological Perspective*. Grand Rapids: Baker Academic, 2014.

Middleton, J. Richard. *The Liberating Image: The* Imago Dei *in Genesis 1*. Grand Rapids: Brazos, 2005.

Milgrom, Jacob. *Leviticus 1–16: A New Translation with Introduction and Commentary*. Anchor Bible 3. New York: Doubleday, 1991.

Moberly, R. W. L. *The Bible, Theology, and Faith: A Study of Abraham and Jesus*. New York: Cambridge University Press, 2000.

Moo, Douglas. *The Epistle to the Romans*. New International Commentary on the New Testament. Grand Rapids: Eerdmans, 1996.

Murphy, Nancey C., Brad J. Kallenberg and Mark Nation, eds. *Virtues & Practices in the Christian Tradition: Christian Ethics After MacIntyre*. Harrisburg, PA: Trinity, 1997.

Muthiah, Robert A. *The Priesthood of All Believers in the Twenty-First Century: Living Faithfully as the Whole People of God in a Postmodern Context*. Eugene, OR: Wipf & Stock, 2009.

Newbigin, Lesslie. *The Gospel in a Pluralistic Society*. Grand Rapids: Eerdmans, 1989.

———. "Ministry and Laity." *National Christian Council Review* 85 (1965): 479-83.

———. *The Open Secret: An Introduction to the Theology of Mission*. Grand Rapids: Eerdmans, 1995.

———. *Unfinished Agenda: An Updated Autobiography*. Grand Rapids: Eerdmans, 1993.

Niebuhr, Reinhold. *The Nature and Destiny of Man: A Christian Interpretation*. 2 vols. London: Nisbet, 1949.

Noll, Ray Robert. *Christian Ministerial Priesthood: A Search for Its Beginnings in the Primary Documents of the Apostolic Fathers*. San Francisco: Catholic Scholars Press, 1993.

Öberg, Ingemar. *Luther and World Mission: A Historical and Systematic Study with Special Reference to Luther's Bible Exposition*.

Translated by Dean Apel. St. Louis: Concordia, 2007.

O'Collins, Gerald, and Michael Keenan Jones. *Jesus Our Priest: A Christian Approach to the Priesthood of Christ.* Oxford: Oxford University Press, 2010.

Oden, Thomas C. *Corrective Love: The Power of Communion Discipline.* St. Louis: Concordia, 1995.

Olson, Roger E., and Christopher A. Hall. *The Trinity.* Guides to Theology. Grand Rapids: Eerdmans, 2002.

Origen. *Homilies on Leviticus: 1–16.* Translated by Gary Barkley. Fathers of the Church 83. Washington, DC: Catholic University of America Press, 1990.

Osborne, Grant R. *Revelation.* Baker Exegetical Commentary on the New Testament. Grand Rapids: Baker, 2002.

Oswalt, John N. *The Book of Isaiah: Chapters 40–66.* New International Commentary on the Old Testament. Grand Rapids: Eerdmans, 1998.

Owen, John. *Communion with the Triune God.* Edited by Kelly M. Kapic and Justin Taylor. Wheaton, IL: Crossway, 2007.

Owens, L. Roger. *The Shape of Participation: A Theology of Church Practices.* Eugene, OR: Cascade, 2010.

Packer, J. I. "A Puritan Perspective: Trinitarian Godliness According to John Owen." In *God the Holy Trinity: Reflections on Christian Faith and Practice,* edited by Timothy George, 91-108. Grand Rapids: Baker Academic, 2006.

Patrick, Dale. "The Covenant Code Source." *Vetus Testamentum* 27 (1977): 145-57.

Pelikan, Jaroslav. "Once for All the Sacrifice of Himself (Heb 9:26)." In *Luther the Expositor,* 237-60. St. Louis: Concordia, 1959.

———. *Spirit Versus Structure: Luther and the Institutions of the Church.* New York: Harper & Row, 1968.

Perrin, Nicholas. *Jesus the Temple.* Grand Rapids: Baker Academic, 2010.

Peterson, David. *Engaging with God: A Biblical Theology of Worship.* Downers Grove, IL: IVP Academic, 1992.

Preus, Herman A. "Luther and the Universal Priesthood and the Office of the Ministry." *Concordia Journal* 5 (1979): 55-62.

Reardon, Patrick Henry. *Christ in the Psalms*. Ben Lomond, CA: Conciliar Press, 2000.

Redding, Graham. *Prayer and the Priesthood of Christ: In the Reformed Tradition*. New York: T&T Clark, 2003.

Roldán, Alberto. "The Priesthood of All Believers and Integral Mission." In *The Local Church, Agent of Transformation: An Ecclesiology for Integral Mission*, edited by Tetsunao Yamamori and C. René Padilla, translated by Brian Cordingly. Buenos Aires: Kairós, 2004.

Romero, Oscar A., and Henri Nouwen. *The Violence of Love*. Translated by James R. Brockman. Maryknoll, NY: Orbis Books, 2004.

Sabourin, Leopold. *Priesthood: A Comparative Study*. Studies in the History of Religions (supplement to Numen) 25. Leiden: Brill, 1973.

Sanders, Fred. *The Deep Things of God: How the Trinity Changes Everything*. Wheaton, IL: Crossway, 2010.

Sanneh, Lamin O. *Translating the Message: The Missionary Impact on Culture*. Maryknoll, NY: Orbis, 2009.

Santantoni, Antonio. "Ordination and Ministries in the West." In *Handbook for Liturgical Studies: Sacraments and Sacramentals*. Edited by Anscar J. Chupungco. Collegeville, MN: Liturgical, 2000.

Sarna, Nahum. *Exodus*. Jewish Publication Society Torah Commentary. New York: Jewish Publication Society, 1991.

Schleiermacher, Friedrich. *The Christian Faith*. Edited by Hugh Ross Mackintosh and J. S. Stewart. New York: T&T Clark, 1928.

Scholer, John M. *Proleptic Priests: Priesthood in the Epistle to the Hebrews*. Journal for the Study of the New Testament: Supplement Series 49. Sheffield: Sheffield Academic, 1991.

Segura C., Harold. "La Misión Como Liberación Integral: Jesús, Modelo Sin Igual." *Kairós* 38 (2006): 23-40.

Silva, Moisés. *Philippians*. 2nd ed. Baker Exegetical Commentary on the New Testament. Grand Rapids: Baker, 2008.

Smith, Gary. *Isaiah 40–66*. Nashville, TN: B&H Academic, 2009.

Smith, Gordon T. *A Holy Meal: The Lord's Supper in the Life of the*

Church. Grand Rapids: Baker Academic, 2005.

Smith, Joseph Fielding. *Doctrines of Salvation: Sermons and Writings of Joseph Fielding Smith*. Edited by Bruce R. McConkie. Salt Lake City, UT: Bookcraft, 1954.

Snyder, Howard A. *The Community of the King*. Downers Grove, IL: IVP Academic, 2004.

Stott, John R. W. *Confess Your Sins: The Way of Reconciliation*. Waco, TX: Word, 1965.

Tanner, Kathryn. "The Trinity." In *The Blackwell Companion to Political Theology*, edited by Peter Scott and William T. Cavanaugh. Blackwell Companions to Religion. Oxford: Blackwell, 2006.

Thomson, John A. F. *The Western Church in the Middle Ages*. London: Arnold, 1998.

Tierney, Brian. *The Crisis of Church & State 1050–1300*. Englewood Cliffs, NJ: Prentice-Hall, 1964.

Torrance, Thomas F. *The Christian Doctrine of God, One Being Three Persons*. Reprint ed. New York: T&T Clark, 2001.

——. *Royal Priesthood: A Theology of Ordained Ministry*. 2nd ed. New York: T&T Clark, 1993.

——. "Service in Jesus Christ." In *Service in Christ: Essays Presented to Karl Barth on His 80th Birthday*, edited by James I. McCord and T. H. L. Parker, 1-16. Grand Rapids: Eerdmans, 1966.

Torrey, R. A. *The Person and Work of the Holy Spirit*. Grand Rapids: Zondervan, 1974.

Tutu, Desmond. *No Future Without Forgiveness*. New York: Doubleday, 2000.

Vajta, Vilmos. *Luther on Worship: An Interpretation*. Eugene, OR: Wipf & Stock, 2004.

Vanhoozer, Kevin J. "Triune Discourse: Theological Reflections on the Claim That God Speaks." In *Trinitarian Theology for the Church: Scripture, Community, Worship*, edited by Daniel J. Treier and David Lauber, 25-78. Downers Grove, IL: IVP Academic, 2009.

Volf, Miroslav. "Theology for a Way of Life." In *Practicing Theology: Beliefs and Practices in Christian Life*, edited by Miroslav Volf and

Dorothy C. Bass, 245-63. Grand Rapids: Eerdmans, 2002.

Voss, Hank. "From 'Grammatical-Historical Exegesis' to 'Theological Exegesis': Five Essential Practices." *Evangelical Review of Theology* 37 (2013): 140-52.

Wainwright, Geoffrey. *Eucharist and Eschatology.* 3rd ed. Peterborough: Epworth, 2002.

Walton, John H. *Genesis.* NIV Application Commentary. Grand Rapids: Zondervan, 2001.

———. *The Lost World of Adam and Eve: Genesis 2–3 and the Human Origins Debate.* Downers Grove, IL: IVP Academic, 2015.

———. *The Lost World of Genesis One: Ancient Cosmology and the Origins Debate.* Downers Grove, IL: IVP Academic, 2009.

Ware, James. *The Mission of the Church in Paul's Letter to the Philippians in the Context of Ancient Judaism.* Boston: Brill, 2005.

Wenham, Gordon J. *Genesis 1–15.* Word Biblical Commentary 1. Waco, TX: Word, 1987.

———. "Sanctuary Symbolism in the Garden of Eden Story." In *I Studied Inscriptions from Before the Flood: Ancient Near Eastern, Literary, and Linguistic Approaches to Genesis 1–11*, edited by Richard S. Hess and David Toshio Tsumura, 399-406. Sources for Biblical and Theological Study 4. Winona Lakes, IN: Eisenbrauns, 1994.

Westcott, Brooke Foss. *The Epistle to the Hebrews.* Grand Rapids: Eerdmans, 1950.

Willard, Dallas. *Renovation of the Heart: Putting on the Character of Christ.* Colorado Springs, CO: NavPress, 2002.

Wilson, Jonathan R. *Living Faithfully in a Fragmented World: Lessons for the Church from MacIntyre's After Virtue.* Harrisburg, PA: Trinity, 1997.

———. *Why Church Matters: Worship, Ministry, and Mission in Practice.* Grand Rapids: Brazos, 2006.

Winter, Ralph. "Two Structures of God's Redemptive Mission." In *Perspectives on the World Christian Movement: Reader*, edited by Ralph D. Winter and Steven C. Hawthorne, 220-30. 3rd ed. Pasadena, CA: William Carey Library, 1999.

Wood, Susan K. *One Baptism: Ecumenical Dimensions of the Doctrine of Baptism.* Collegeville, MN: Liturgical, 2009.

Wright, Christopher J. H. "The World in the Bible." *Evangelical Review of Theology* 34, no. 3 (2010): 207-19.

Wright, N. T. *After You Believe: Why Christian Character Matters.* New York: HarperCollins, 2010.

Yoder, John Howard. *The Fullness of Christ: Paul's Revolutionary Vision of Universal Ministry.* Elgin, IL: Brethren, 1987.

Zizioulas, John D. *Being as Communion: Studies in Personhood and the Church.* Crestwood, NY: St. Vladimir's Seminary Press, 1985.

Name and Subject Index

Scripture Index

Finding the Textbook You Need

The IVP Academic Textbook Selector
is an online tool for instantly finding the IVP books
suitable for over 250 courses across 24 disciplines.

ivpacademic.com